1	+	5	=	6
2	+	5	=	7
3	+	5	=	8
4	+	5	=	9
5	+	5	=	10
6	+	5	=	11
7	+	5	=	12
8	+	5	=	13
9	+	5	=	14
10	+	5	=	15
11	+	5	=	16
12	+	5	=	17

1				
2	+	6	=	8
3	+	6	=	9
4	+	6	=	10
5	+	6	=	11
6	+	6	=	12
7	+	6	=	13
8	+	6	=	14
9	+	6	=	15
10	+	6	=	16
11	+	6	=	17
12	+	6	=	18

1	+	7	=	8
2	+	7	=	9
3	+	7	=	10
4	+	7	=	11
5	+	7	=	12
6	+	7	=	13
7	+	7	=	14
8	+	7	=	15
9	+	7	=	16
10	+	7	=	17
11	+	7	=	18
12	+	7	=	19

1	+	8	=	9
2	+	8	=	10
3	+	8	=	11
4	+	8	=	12
5	+	8	=	13
6	+	8	=	14
7	+	8	=	15
8	+	8	=	16
9	+	8	=	17
10	+	8	=	18
11	+	8	=	19
12	+	8	=	20

1	+	9	=	10		1	+	10	=	11
2	+	9	=	11		2	+	10	=	12
3	+	9	=	12		3	+	10	=	13
4	+	9	=	13		4	+	10	=	14
5	+	9	=	14		5	+	10	=	15
6	+	9	=	15		6	+	10	=	16
7	+	9	=	16		7	+	10	=	17
8	+	9	=	17		8	+	10	=	18
9	+	9	=	18		9	+	10	=	19
10	+	9	=	19		10	+	10	=	20
11	+	9	=	20		11	+	10	=	21
12	+	9	=	21		12	+	10	=	22

1	+	11	=	12		1	+	12	=	13
2	+	11	=	13		2	+	12	=	14
3	+	11	=	14		3	+	12	=	15
4	+	11	=	15		4	+	12	=	16
5	+	11	=	16		5	+	12	=	17
6	+	11	=	17		6	+	12	=	18
7	+	11	=	18		7	+	12	=	19
8	+	11	=	19		8	+	12	=	20
9	+	11	=	20		9	+	12	=	21
10	+	11	=	21		10	+	12	=	22
11	+	11	=	22		11	+	12	=	23
12	+	11	=	23		12	+	12	=	24

Elephant math

Do the addition and write the answers on the buckets.

6 + 2 = 8

4 + 4 = 8

3 + 7 = 10

Addition on the farm

Complete the problems.

$4 + \boxed{4} = 8$

$\boxed{5} + 7 = 12$

$7 + \boxed{7} = 14$

$4 + 3 = \boxed{7}$

$\boxed{12} + 6 = 18$

$9 + \boxed{7} = 16$

$11 + 5 = \boxed{16}$

$\boxed{12} + 8 = 20$

$8 + 8 = \boxed{16}$

$12 + \boxed{12} = 24$

$\boxed{7} + 8 = 15$

$10 + 3 = \boxed{13}$

$9 + \boxed{9} = 18$

$12 + \boxed{10} = 22$

$11 + 3 = \boxed{14}$

$\boxed{6} + 6 = 13$

X

$$11 + 11 = 22$$
$$7 + 26 = 19$$
$$4 + 3 = 7$$
$$22 + 11 = 11$$
$$8 + 29 = 21$$
$$20 + 3 = 23$$
$$32 + 3 = 35$$

WATCH

$$18 + 12 = 30$$
$$12 + 12 = 24$$
$$1 + 9 = 10$$
$$10 + 10 = 20$$
$$7 + 9 = 16$$
$$2 + 2 = 4$$
$$8 + 2 = 10$$

Missing numbers

Count the objects to complete the problems.

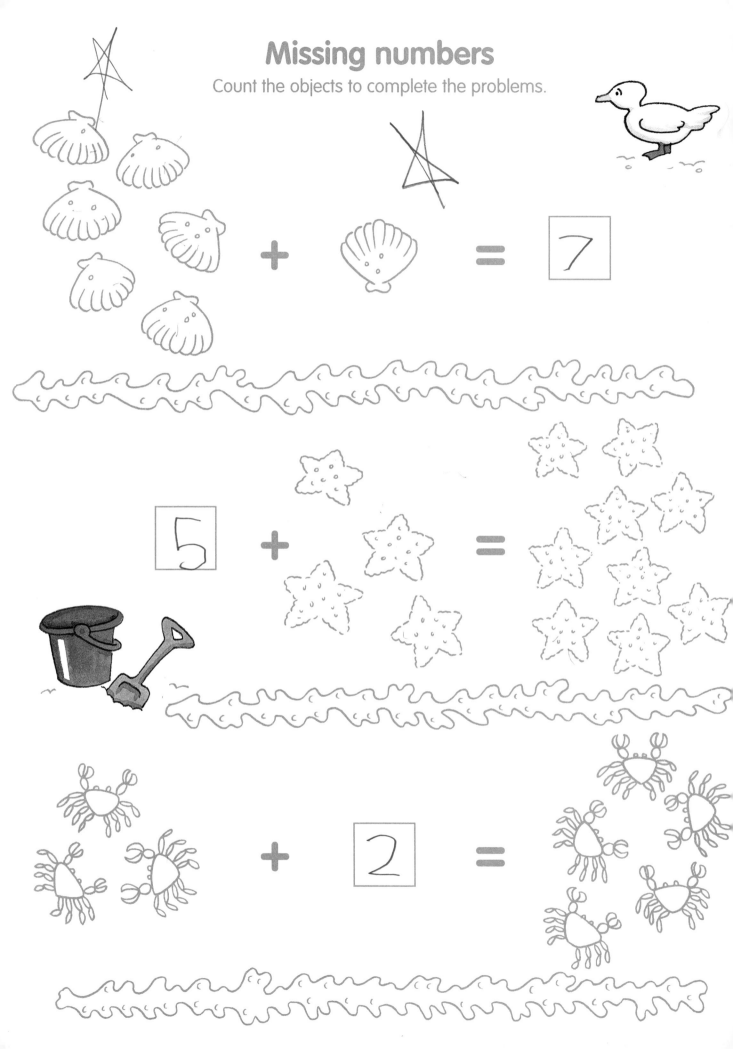

$+$ $=$ $\boxed{7}$

$\boxed{5}$ $+$ $=$

$+$ $\boxed{2}$ $=$

Window math

Do the addition and write the answers on the windows.

3	+	5	=	8	
3	+	12	=	2	check
5	+	5	=	10	
9	+	6	=	15	

Kite math

Count the bows on the kites.
Do the addition and draw the number of bows on the last kite.

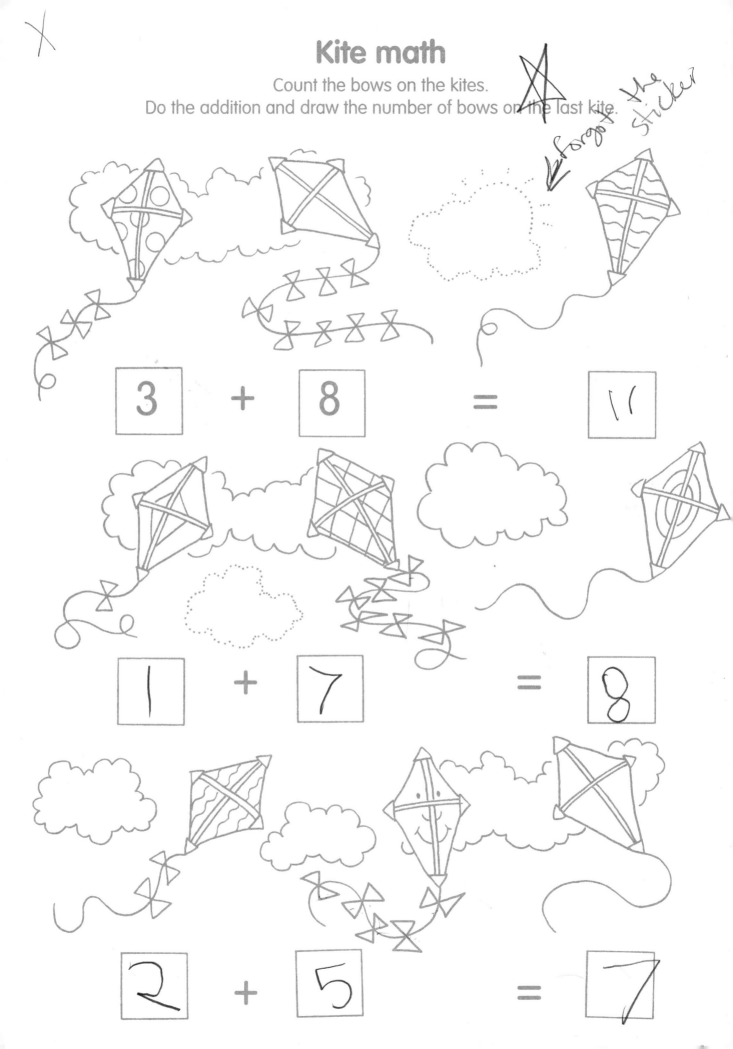

forgot the sticker

3 + 8 = 11

1 + 7 = 8

2 + 5 = 7

Balloon math

The answers to the problems on the balloons are printed on the children's T-shirts.
Draw a line to connect each balloon to the correct child.

Number puzzles

Complete the problems in the grids by filling in the missing numbers.

X

Redo

$8 + \square = 11$

4	+	8	=	12
+		+		+
1	+	1	=	2
=		=		=
5	+	11	=	16

$12 + \square = 16$

11	+	9	=	20
+		+		+
2	+	2	=	4
=		=		=
1	+	11	=	12

$20 + 4 = \square$

$11 + 2 = \square$

$\square + 11 = 24$

Number crossword

Do the addition. Write the answers as words in the crossword grid.
Use the words in the box below to help you.

a. 6 + 6 = 12
a. 2 + 0 = 2
b. 3 + 7 = 10
c. 9 + 2 = 11

d. 3 + 1 = 4
e. 1 + 0 = 1
f. 2 + 1 = 3
g. 5 + 3 = 8

Word box:
~~ten~~
eight
three
~~twelve~~
~~eleven~~
~~four~~
~~two~~
~~one~~

Number lines

Do the addition and write the answers on the hot-air balloons.
Draw a line to connect each answer to its place on the number line.

5 + 5 = 10

2 + 2 =
4

3 + 2 =
5

4 + 5 =
9

6 + 1 =
7

0   1   2   3   4   5   6   7   8   9   10

Match the answers

Draw a line to connect the problem on each sailboat to its answer on the anchor.

7 + 7 =

8 + 8 =

11 + 11 =

10 + 10 =

16

20

14

22

Addition test

Do the addition and write the answers in the boxes.

$11 + 2 = \boxed{13}$

$6 + 7 = \boxed{13}$

$10 + 5 = \boxed{15}$

$6 + 9 = \boxed{15}$

$3 + 12 = \boxed{15}$

$2 + 8 = \boxed{10}$

$7 + 5 = \boxed{12}$

$5 + 5 = \boxed{10}$

$8 + 8 = \boxed{16}$

$10 + 3 = \boxed{13}$

$2 + 2 = \boxed{4}$

$4 + 5 = \boxed{9}$

$5 + 9 = \boxed{14}$

$$1 + 9 = \boxed{10}$$

$$3 + 3 = \boxed{6}$$

$$6 + 6 = \boxed{12}$$

$$4 + 7 = \boxed{11}$$

$$9 + 6 = \boxed{15}$$

$$11 + 11 = \boxed{22}$$

$$7 + 12 = \boxed{19}$$

$$3 + 9 = \boxed{12}$$

$$4 + 2 = \boxed{6}$$

$$12 + 4 = \boxed{16}$$

$$8 + 4 = \boxed{12}$$

Subtraction tables

Learn the subtraction tables and remember them.

2 - 1 = 1		3 - 2 = 1
3 - 1 = 2		4 - 2 = 2
4 - 1 = 3		5 - 2 = 3
5 - 1 = 4		6 - 2 = 4
6 - 1 = 5		7 - 2 = 5
7 - 1 = 6		8 - 2 = 6
8 - 1 = 7		9 - 2 = 7
9 - 1 = 8		10 - 2 = 8
10 - 1 = 9		11 - 2 = 9
11 - 1 = 10		12 - 2 = 10
12 - 1 = 11		13 - 2 = 11
13 - 1 = 12		14 - 2 = 12

4 - 3 = 1		5 - 4 = 1
5 - 3 = 2		6 - 4 = 2
6 - 3 = 3		7 - 4 = 3
7 - 3 = 4		8 - 4 = 4
8 - 3 = 5		9 - 4 = 5
9 - 3 = 6		10 - 4 = 6
10 - 3 = 7		11 - 4 = 7
11 - 3 = 8		12 - 4 = 8
12 - 3 = 9		13 - 4 = 9
13 - 3 = 10		14 - 4 = 10
14 - 3 = 11		15 - 4 = 11
15 - 3 = 12		16 - 4 = 12

6 - 5 = 1		7 - 6 = 1
7 - 5 = 2		8 - 6 = 2
8 - 5 = 3		9 - 6 = 3
9 - 5 = 4		10 - 6 = 4
10 - 5 = 5		11 - 6 = 5
11 - 5 = 6		12 - 6 = 6
12 - 5 = 7		13 - 6 = 7
13 - 5 = 8		14 - 6 = 8
14 - 5 = 9		15 - 6 = 9
15 - 5 = 10		16 - 6 = 10
16 - 5 = 11		17 - 6 = 11
17 - 5 = 12		18 - 6 = 12

8 - 7 = 1		9 - 8 = 1
9 - 7 = 2		10 - 8 = 2
10 - 7 = 3		11 - 8 = 3
11 - 7 = 4		12 - 8 = 4
12 - 7 = 5		13 - 8 = 5
13 - 7 = 6		14 - 8 = 6
14 - 7 = 7		15 - 8 = 7
15 - 7 = 8		16 - 8 = 8
16 - 7 = 9		17 - 8 = 9
17 - 7 = 10		18 - 8 = 10
18 - 7 = 11		19 - 8 = 11
19 - 7 = 12		20 - 8 = 12

10	-	9	=	1
11	-	9	=	2
12	-	9	=	3
13	-	9	=	4
14	-	9	=	5
15	-	9	=	6
16	-	9	=	7
17	-	9	=	8
18	-	9	=	9
19	-	9	=	10
20	-	9	=	11
21	-	9	=	12

11	-	10	=	1
12	-	10	=	2
13	-	10	=	3
14	-	10	=	4
15	-	10	=	5
16	-	10	=	6
17	-	10	=	7
18	-	10	=	8
19	-	10	=	9
20	-	10	=	10
21	-	10	=	11
22	-	10	=	12

12	-	11	=	1
13	-	11	=	2
14	-	11	=	3
15	-	11	=	4
16	-	11	=	5
17	-	11	=	6
18	-	11	=	7
19	-	11	=	8
20	-	11	=	9
21	-	11	=	10
22	-	11	=	11
23	-	11	=	12

13	-	12	=	1
14	-	12	=	2
15	-	12	=	3
16	-	12	=	4
17	-	12	=	5
18	-	12	=	6
19	-	12	=	7
20	-	12	=	8
21	-	12	=	9
22	-	12	=	10
23	-	12	=	11
24	-	12	=	12

Penguin math

Do the subtraction and write the answers on the penguins.

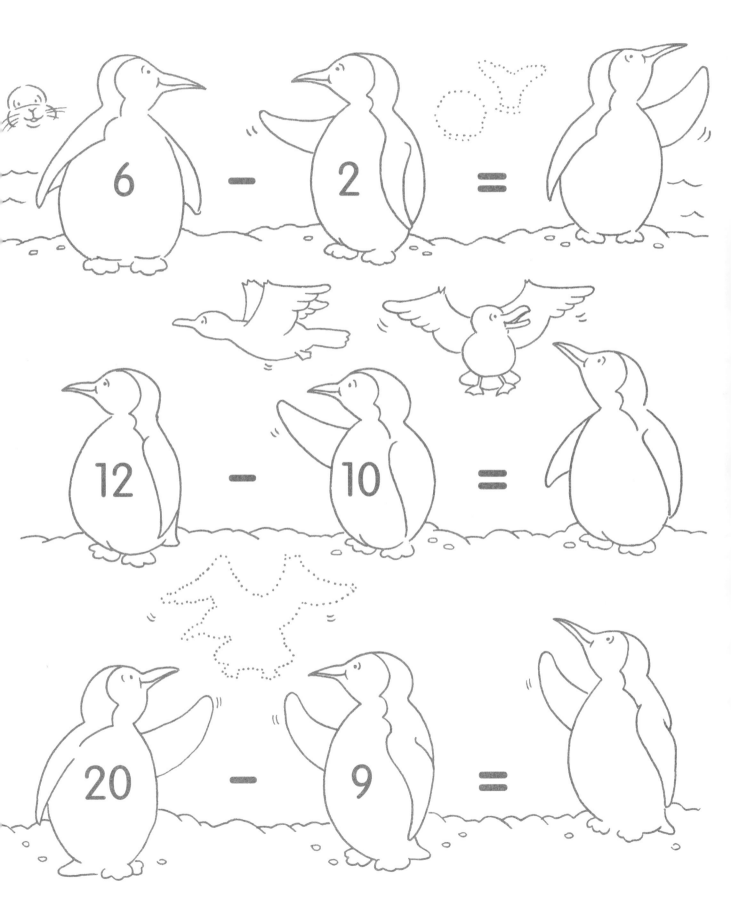

6 − 2 =

12 − 10 =

20 − 9 =

Subtraction in space

Complete the problems.

3 − ☐ = 0

☐ − 4 = 8

21 − ☐ = 14

15 − 5 = ☐

☐ − 6 = 18

14 − ☐ = 12

9 − 1 = ☐

☐ − 2 = 16

16 − 7 = ☐

24 − ☐ = 24

☐ − 9 = 0

18 − 10 = ☐

22 − ☐ = 11

9 − ☐ = 6

12 − 4 = ☐

☐ − 7 = 15

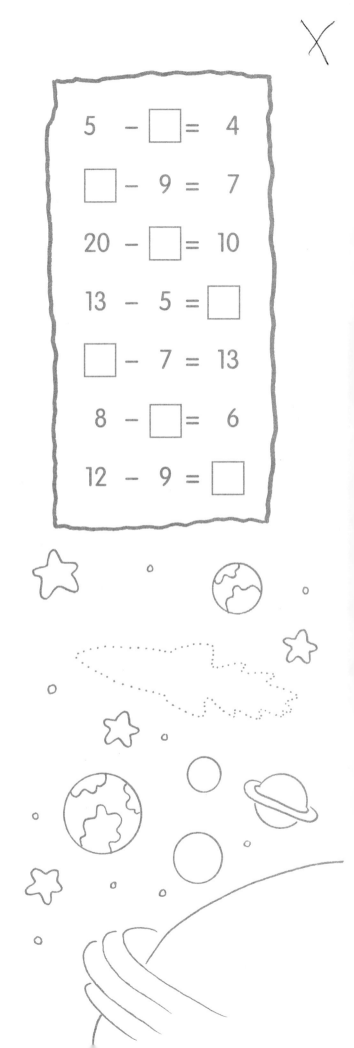

$5 - \boxed{} = 4$

$\boxed{} - 9 = 7$

$20 - \boxed{} = 10$

$13 - 5 = \boxed{}$

$\boxed{} - 7 = 13$

$8 - \boxed{} = 6$

$12 - 9 = \boxed{}$

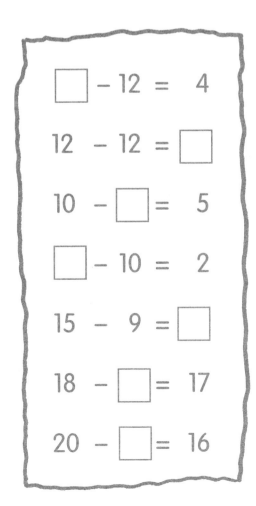

$\boxed{} - 12 = 4$

$12 - 12 = \boxed{}$

$10 - \boxed{} = 5$

$\boxed{} - 10 = 2$

$15 - 9 = \boxed{}$

$18 - \boxed{} = 17$

$20 - \boxed{} = 16$

Bubble math

Complete the problems in the bubbles by filling in the missing numbers.

10 − 5 = ◯

12 − 7 = ◯

8 − 3 = ◯

12 − ◯ = 7

◯ − ◯ = 3 = 9

14 − 5 = ◯

Fun with subtraction

Solve these problems.

Take 4 bananas away from these monkeys.
How many bananas are left?

If 3 parrots fly away, how many parrots are left?

Color 6 of the crocodile's teeth. How many teeth are left white?

Two rabbits eat 2 carrots each.
How many carrots are left?

Draw 8 lighted candles on this cake.
If the boy blows out 3 candles,
how many lighted candles are left?

Which is right?

Circle the problems whose answers match
the numbers at the top of each box.

18
10 – 7
33 – 12
15 – 3
27 – 9

40
25 – 5
50 – 10
48 – 6
10 – 5

24
30 – 6
42 – 7
64 – 8
20 – 2

21
45 – 5
21 – 7
30 – 9
10 – 4

10
5 – 5
10 – 1
12 – 2
18 – 7

8
88 – 10
16 – 8
12 – 6
72 – 9

Subtraction wordsearch

Do the subtraction and write the answers in the boxes.
Look for the written answers in the wordsearch grid.
You will find them by reading across and down.
Circle the words as you find them.

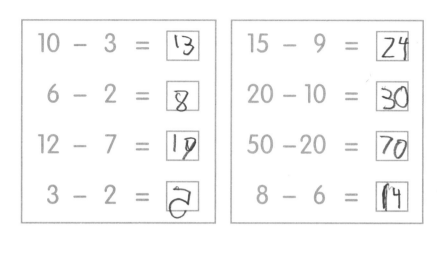

10 − 3 =	13	15 − 9 =	24
6 − 2 =	8	20 − 10 =	30
12 − 7 =	10	50 − 20 =	70
3 − 2 =	2	8 − 6 =	14

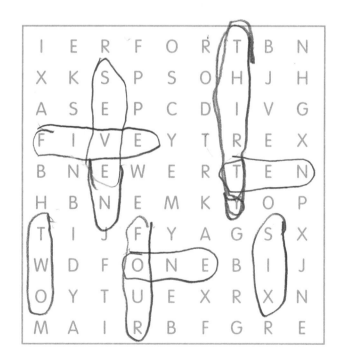

```
I  E  R  F  O  R  T  B  N
X  K  S  P  S  O  H  J  H
A  S  E  P  C  D  I  V  G
F  I  V  E  Y  T  R  E  X
B  N  E  W  E  R  T  E  N
H  B  N  E  M  K  T  O  P
T  I  J  F  Y  A  G  S  X
W  D  F  O  N  E  B  I  J
O  Y  T  U  E  X  R  X  N
M  A  I  R  B  F  G  R  E
```

Subtraction test

Do the subtraction and write the answers in the boxes.

8 − 4 = ☐

12 − 2 = ☐

17 − 5 = ☐

20 − 9 = ☐

9 − 1 = ☐

13 − 5 = ☐

24 − 12 = ☐

5 − 5 = ☐

11 − 3 = ☐

20 − 12 = ☐

10 − 4 = ☐

23 − 11 = ☐

13 − 8 = ☐

11 − 1 = ☐

15 − 9 = ☐

3 − 3 = ☐

18 − 6 = ☐

7 − 2 = ☐

16 − 6 = ☐

15 − 5 = ☐

17 − 3 = ☐

7 − 3 = ☐

14 − 12 = ☐

17 − 8 = ☐

Answers

Elephant math
$6 + 2 = 8$ $4 + 4 = 8$ $3 + 7 = 10$

Addition on the farm
$4 + 4 = 8$ $5 + 7 = 12$ $7 + 7 = 14$
$4 + 3 = 7$ $12 + 6 = 18$ $9 + 7 = 16$
$11 + 5 = 16$ $12 + 8 = 20$ $8 + 8 = 16$
$12 + 12 = 24$ $7 + 8 = 15$ $10 + 3 = 13$
$9 + 9 = 18$ $12 + 10 = 22$ $11 + 3 = 14$
$7 + 6 = 13$ $11 + 11 = 22$ $7 + 12 = 19$
$4 + 3 = 7$ $0 + 11 = 11$ $8 + 13 = 21$
$20 + 3 = 23$ $32 + 3 = 35$ $18 + 12 = 30$
$12 + 12 = 24$ $1 + 9 = 10$ $10 + 10 = 20$
$7 + 9 = 16$ $2 + 2 = 4$ $8 + 2 = 10$

Missing numbers
$6 + 1 = 7$ $5 + 4 = 9$ $3 + 2 = 5$

Window math
$3 + 5 = 8$ $3 + 12 = 15$ $5 + 5 = 10$
$9 + 6 = 15$

Kite math
$3 + 8 = 11$ $1 + 6 = 7$ $2 + 5 = 7$

Balloon math
$8 + 11 = 19$ $9 + 9 = 18$ $12 + 10 = 22$

Number puzzles

4	+	8	=	12
+		+		+
1	+	3	=	4
=		=		=
5	+	11	=	16

11	+	9	=	20
+		+		+
2	+	2	=	4
=		=		=
13	+	11	=	24

Number crossword

		²t	w	o		
		w			⁵t	
		⁴e	l	e	v	e	n
					l	
³f				i	v	
°o	n	e			
	u				
¹t	h	r	⁶e	e	
			i	
			g	
			h	
			t	

Number lines
$5 + 5 = 10$ $2 + 2 = 4$ $3 + 2 = 5$
$4 + 5 = 9$ $6 + 1 = 7$

Match the answers
$7 + 7 = 14$ $8 + 8 = 16$
$11 + 11 = 22$ $10 + 10 = 20$

Addition test
$11 + 2 = 13$ $6 + 7 = 13$ $10 + 5 = 15$
$6 + 9 = 15$ $3 + 12 = 15$ $2 + 8 = 10$
$7 + 5 = 12$ $5 + 5 = 10$ $8 + 8 = 16$
$10 + 3 = 13$ $2 + 2 = 4$ $4 + 5 = 9$
$5 + 9 = 14$ $1 + 9 = 10$ $3 + 3 = 6$
$6 + 6 = 12$ $4 + 7 = 11$ $9 + 6 = 15$
$11 + 11 = 22$ $7 + 12 = 19$ $3 + 9 = 12$
$4 + 2 = 6$ $12 + 4 = 16$ $8 + 4 = 12$

Penguin math
$6 - 2 = 4$ $12 - 10 = 2$ $20 - 9 = 11$

Subtraction in space
$3 - 3 = 0$ $12 - 4 = 8$ $21 - 7 = 14$
$15 - 5 = 10$ $24 - 6 = 18$ $14 - 2 = 12$
$9 - 1 = 8$ $18 - 2 = 16$ $16 - 7 = 9$
$24 - 0 = 24$ $9 - 9 = 0$ $18 - 10 = 8$
$22 - 11 = 11$ $9 - 3 = 6$ $12 - 4 = 8$
$22 - 7 = 15$ $5 - 1 = 4$ $16 - 9 = 7$
$20 - 10 = 10$ $13 - 5 = 8$ $20 - 7 = 13$
$8 - 2 = 6$ $12 - 9 = 3$ $16 - 12 = 4$
$12 - 12 = 0$ $10 - 5 = 5$ $12 - 10 = 2$
$15 - 9 = 6$ $18 - 1 = 17$ $20 - 4 = 16$

Bubble math
$10 - 5 = 5$ $12 - 7 = 5$ $8 - 3 = 5$
$12 - 5 = 7$ $12 - 3 = 9$ $14 - 5 = 9$

Fun with subtraction
2 bananas, 4 parrots, 5 teeth, 2 carrots, 5 candles

Which is right?
$27 - 9 = 18$ $50 - 10 = 40$ $30 - 6 = 24$
$30 - 9 = 21$ $12 - 2 = 10$ $16 - 8 = 16$

Subtraction wordsearch

I	E	R	F	O	R	T	B	N
X	K	S	P	S	O	H	J	H
A	S	E	X	C	D	I	V	G
F	I	V	E	Y	T	R	E	X
B	N	E	W	E	R	T	E	N
H	B	N	E	M	K	Y	O	P
T	I	J	F	Y	A	G	S	X
W	D	F	O	N	E	B	I	J
O	Y	T	U	E	X	R	X	N
M	A	I	R	B	F	G	R	E

Subtraction test
$8 - 4 = 4$ $12 - 2 = 10$ $17 - 5 = 12$
$20 - 9 = 11$ $9 - 1 = 8$ $13 - 5 = 8$
$24 - 12 = 12$ $5 - 5 = 0$ $11 - 3 = 8$
$20 - 12 = 8$ $10 - 4 = 6$ $23 - 11 = 12$
$13 - 8 = 5$ $11 - 1 = 10$ $15 - 9 = 6$
$3 - 3 = 0$ $18 - 6 = 12$ $7 - 2 = 5$
$16 - 6 = 10$ $15 - 5 = 10$ $17 - 3 = 14$
$7 - 3 = 4$ $14 - 12 = 2$ $17 - 8 = 9$

Spelling

Especially suitable for grades 1-4

Missing letters

Find the stickers and put them in place.
Fill in the missing letters to complete the words.

_nc_or

_o_t

loc

_o_

_le_hant

_r_g

_o_t

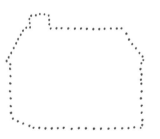

_o_se

glo

p_tch_r

_oa_a

_io_

onke

_e_t

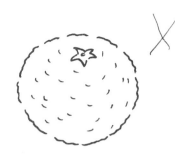
_ran_e

_an_a

_ue_n

_ab_it

_ta_

_i_er

_mbrel_a

_iol_n

_al_us

_ylo_hone

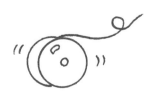
_o-y_

_eb_a

First letters

Find the stickers and put them in place, then complete the words.

_ _ead

_ _own

_ _own

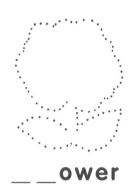

_ _ower

_ _ums

_ _arecrow

_ _ide

_ _ail

_ _ider

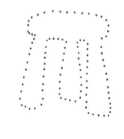

_ _ool

_ _ing

_ _actor

_ _ig

_ _apes

_ _og

_ _incess

Last letters

Find the stickers and put them in place, then complete the words.

si_ _

la_ _

go_ _

frie_ _

te_ _

mi_ _

co_ _

wa_ _

whi_ _

du_ _

thu_ _

a_ _

prese_ _

hea_ _

toa_ _

pai_ _

Letter ladders

Put a check next to the words that are spelled correctly.

always
allways

before
beafore

children
childran

different
diffrent

earth
erth

knew
knewe

leave
leeve

weight
wieght

beacause
because

opened
openned

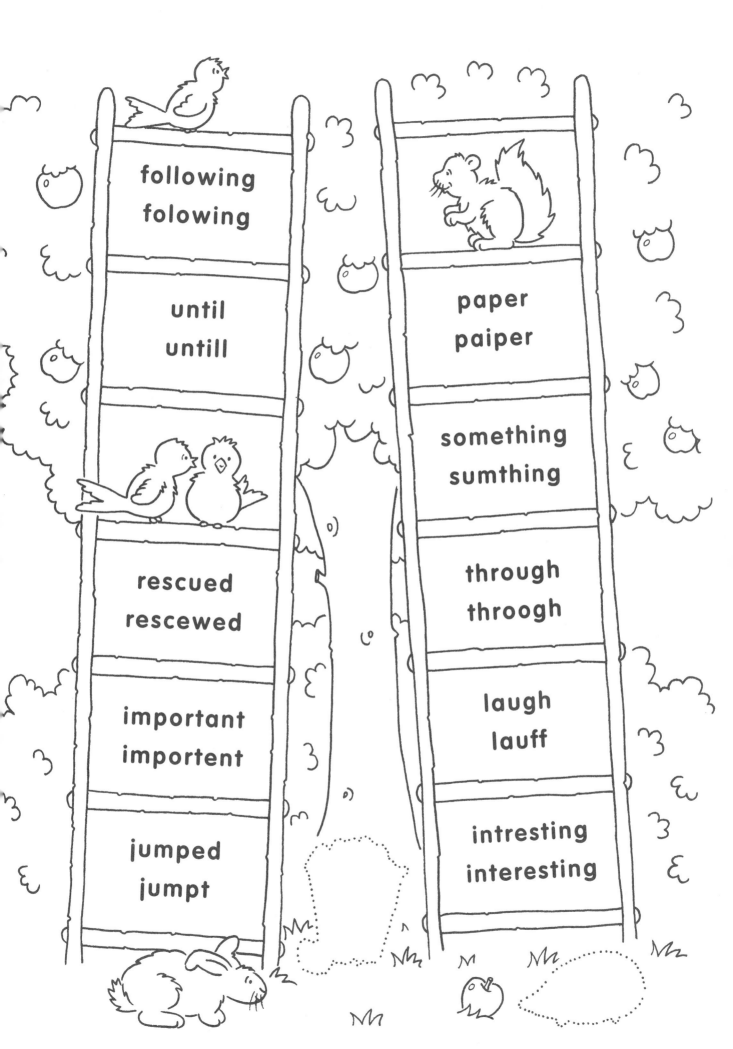

following
folowing

until
untill

rescued
rescewed

important
importent

jumped
jumpt

paper
paiper

something
sumthing

through
throogh

laugh
lauff

intresting
interesting

Days of the week

Fill in the missing letters to spell each day of the week, then complete the sentences.

M _ _ day

I played s_____ after school.

T _ _ _ day

I did my h_____ .

_ ed_ _ _ _ day

I w_____ the dog with my grandpa.

_ _ur_ day

I went s _____ with my friends.

F_ _ _ay

I w_____ television after school.

_ _ _t_ _day

I went s_____ for new c_____ .

S_ _ day

I went on a p_____ with my f_____ .

What day is it today? Spell it.

_____

What day will it be tomorrow? Spell it.

_____

Months of the year

Fill in the missing letters to spell each month of the year, then complete the sentences.

J_a_ua_y

I made a sn_o_wm_an_.

F_e_br___ry

Fl___ers started gr___ing.

_ar___

I fl_b my k_it_e.

Ap_r_l

L_am_bs played in the f_i_ld.

M_a_y

Baby birds sang in their n_es_t.

___n_

I played te_nn_is.

Ju_ly

Augist

S____emb__

I made cas_ll_es in
the sand.

We saw some
do_l_phins.

The le_ff_es fell from
the tr_ee_ s.

__t___er

No_v_em_b_er

De_c_em_ber

My umbr_ell_la
kept me dry.

We ate t_ur_key.

Santa brou_ght me lots
of p_ll_sents.

Spell the month we are in now. _____

Spell the month of your birthday. _____

Number words

Spell the numbers 1 to 20 on these rocketships.
Then spell the other numbers in the cloud of smoke.

Plural endings

Add the plural endings "**s**", "**es**", or "**ies**" to change these spellings.

witch _____   fairy _____

wand _____   cherry _____

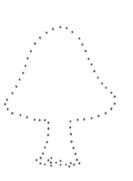   

toadstool _____   box _____

star _____   book _____

Adding a letter

Add a letter to these words to magically change them into different words.
Write the new words in the boxes.

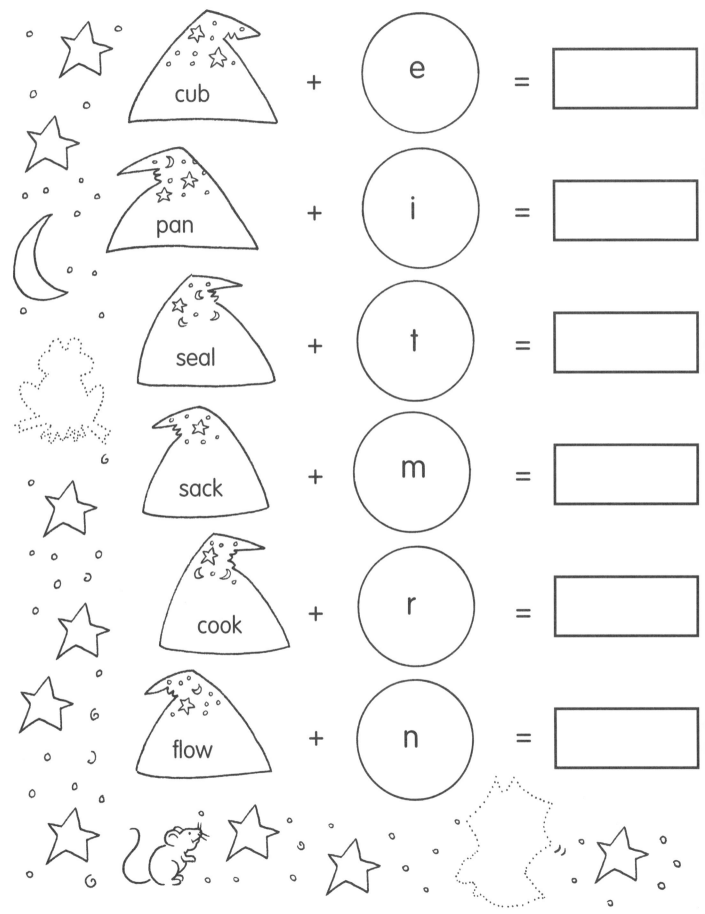

cub + e =

pan + i =

seal + t =

sack + m =

cook + r =

flow + n =

"Magic e" wordsearch

Find the stickers and put them in place. The "magic e" changes the sound of a vowel from a short sound to a long sound. Look at the pictures and find the words in the wordsearch grid. You will find them by reading across and down.
Circle the words as you find them.

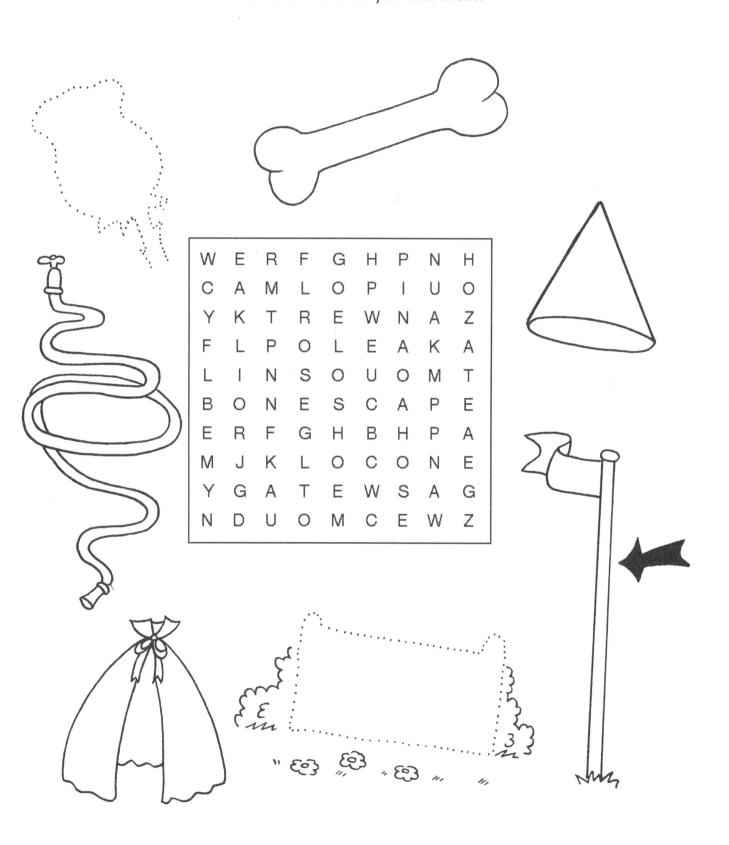

W	E	R	F	G	H	P	N	H
C	A	M	L	O	P	I	U	O
Y	K	T	R	E	W	N	A	Z
F	L	P	O	L	E	A	K	A
L	I	N	S	O	U	O	M	T
B	O	N	E	S	C	A	P	E
E	R	F	G	H	B	H	P	A
M	J	K	L	O	C	O	N	E
Y	G	A	T	E	W	S	A	G
N	D	U	O	M	C	E	W	Z

Vowel vampire

The vowel vampire has gone batty! Complete the words on the coffins
by filling in the missing vowels. The bats are holding the vowels to help you.

e

a

o   u

i

h_gh

br__ght

b_f_r_

m_rn_ng

t_g_th_r

w_nd_w

y__ng

w_th__t

_cr_ss

b_b__s

b_l_w

ch_ng_

m_th_r

g_rd_n

ch_ldr_n

s_st_r

w_rld

_lw_ys

Pumpkin picker

Follow the vowels to help the pumpkin picker through the field to the tractor.

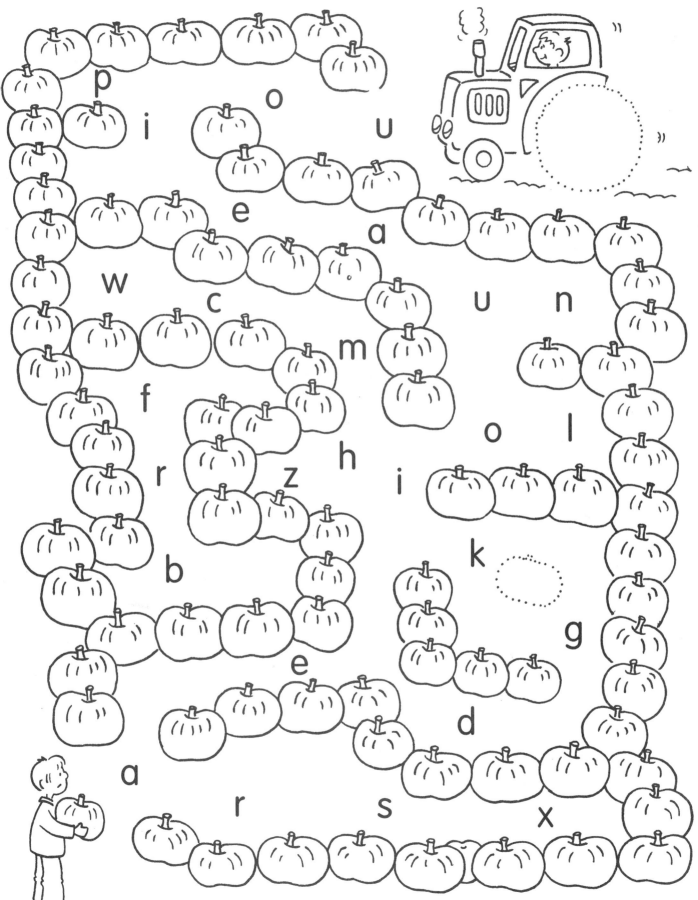

Farm frolics

Complete the words in the speech bubbles by using the following letter sounds:
"ur" "or" "er" "ir".

Rhyme time

Find the stickers and put them in place.
Complete these words by adding the missing vowel sounds.
Draw a line to connect each pair of words that rhyme.

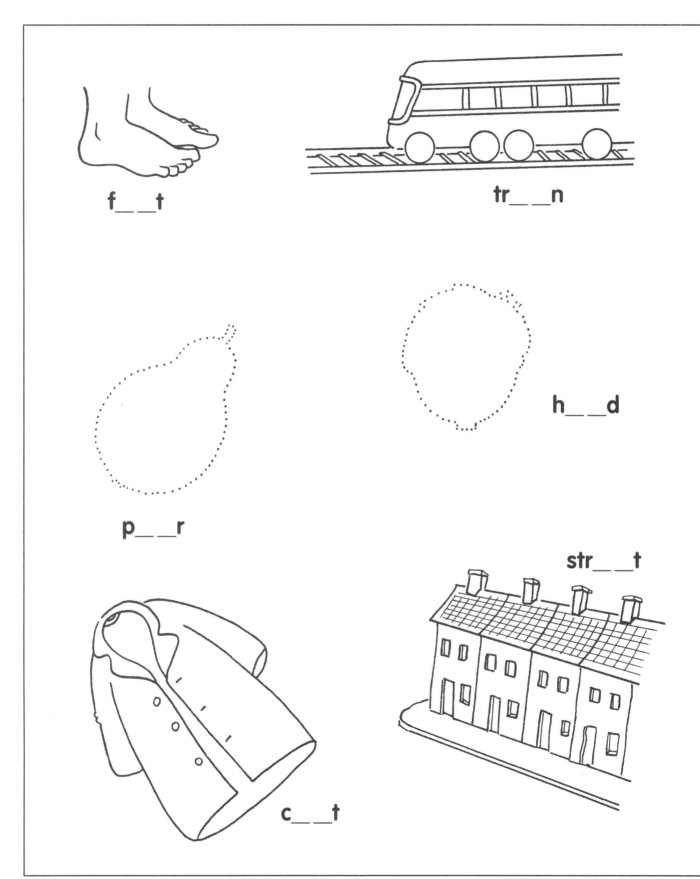

f__t

tr__ __n

h__ __d

p__ __r

str__ __t

c__ __t

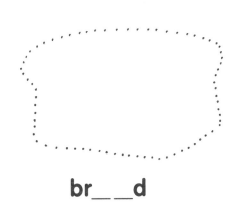

br_ _d

m_ _n

b_ _t

b_ _r

sp_ _n

r_ _n

Crossword

The letters **"ou"** and **"ow"** are different letters that can make the same sound.
Follow the numbers across and down, and write the words in the grid.

Wish you were here

The letters "**ai**" and "**ay**" are different letters that can make the same sound.
Complete this postcard by spelling the missing words.

Dear Anna,
We are st_ _ing in a little
cottage by the ocean.
On Tuesd_ _ we went
s_ _ling around the coast.
It started to r_ _n and we
all got very wet! I pl_ _ed
on the beach and found
lots of sea shells and
sn_ _ls. Wish you were here!
Love,
Gwen

Anna Haynes
101 Sutton Road
Springfield,
IL 62741

Jungle fever

Unscramble the letters in the vines to spell the names of some jungle creatures. Write the words. Use the pictures to help you.

Double trouble

Fill in the missing pairs of letters to spell the words
these twins are holding.

sni___ stu___

bu___ we___

ma___ che___

thri___ sma___

bo___ cro___

 cli___ cu___

 gra___ gla___

 ca___ot pa___ot

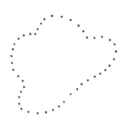

 ho___er sto___er

 ki___en mi___en

Space race

Use the letters in the stars to help you spell the words.

lk

ld

lp

go___en

shou___

he___ing

gu___ing

wou___

cha___

ly   lt   le   ll

mudd___

quick___

me___

lone___

batt___

she___s

Snakes and ladders

If you add "**ing**" or "**ed**" to some verbs, you sometimes have to double a letter.
Add "**ing**" or "**ed**" to these verbs. Write the new words in the ladders.
Don't forget—you may have to double a letter!

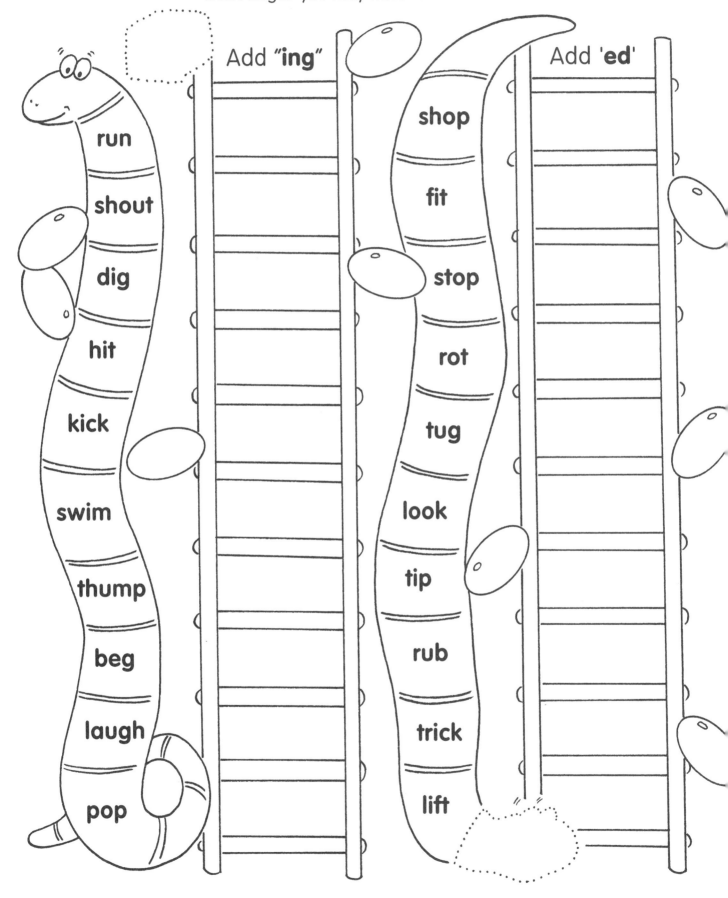

Add "**ing**"

run
shout
dig
hit
kick
swim
thump
beg
laugh
pop

Add '**ed**'

shop
fit
stop
rot
tug
look
tip
rub
trick
lift

"eer", "ere", or "ier"?

Complete these words by adding **"eer"**, **"ere"**, or **"ier"**.

d____

t____

ch____

h____

st____

volunt____

barr____

car____

Answers

Missing letters
anchor boat clock dog elephant frog goat house igloo pitcher koala lion monkey nest orange panda queen rabbit star tiger umbrella violin walrus xylophone yo-yo zebra

First letters
bread clown crown flower plums scarecrow slide snail spider stool swing tractor twig grapes frog princess

Last letters
sink lamb golf friend tent milk comb wasp whisk duck thumb ant present heart toast paint

Letter ladders
always before children different earth knew leave weight because opened following until rescued important jumped paper something through laugh interesting

Days of the week
Monday soccer Tuesday homework Wednesday walked Thursday swimming Friday watched Saturday shopping clothes Sunday picnic family

Months of the year
January snowman February flowers growing March flew kite April lambs field May nest June tennis July castles August dolphins September leaves trees October umbrella November turkey December brought presents

Number words
ten nine eight seven six five four three two one twenty nineteen eighteen seventeen sixteen fifteen fourteen thirteen twelve eleven thirty forty fifty sixty seventy eighty ninety one hundred

Plural endings
witches fairies wands cherries toadstools boxes stars books

Adding a letter
cube pain steal smack crook flown

"Magic e" wordsearch

Vowel vampire
high brought before morning together window young without across babies below change mother garden children sister world always

Farm frolics
word first dirt girl twirl furniture curve modern burst return horror interior mayor sword radiator ladder ever nurse dinner bigger thirsty bird

Rhyme time
feet - street, train - rain, pear - bear, head - bread, coat - boat, moon - spoon

Crossword

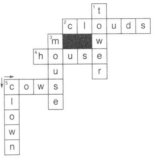

Wish you were here
staying Tuesday sailing rain played snails

Jungle fever
monkey elephant lizard parrot tiger snake lion leopard

Double trouble
sniff, stuff, bull, well, mass, chess, thrill, small, boss, cross, cliff, cuff, grass, glass, carrot, parrot, hopper, stopper, kitten, mitten

Space race
golden should helping gulping would chalk shells muddle quickly melt lonely battle

Snakes and ladders
running shouting digging hitting kicking swimming thumping begging laughing popping shopped fitted stopped rotted tugged looked tipped rubbed tricked lifted

"eer", "ere", or "ier"
deer tier here cheer steer volunteer career barrier

Help with Homework

Reading
and
Writing

Especially suitable for grades 1-4

In town

Fill in the missing letters in these signs.

_AK_RY

GRE_NGR_CER

EAST STR_ _T

_ISH _TORE

REST_UR_NT

A sleepy surprise

This story has gotten mixed up.
Put the story in order by writing the letters in the boxes at the bottom of the page.

A Freddie called his friends over to take a look.

B Suddenly, he noticed a pair of eyes staring at him.

C It was an ordinary morning at the fire house.

D Freddie Fizz was polishing his shiny red fire engine.

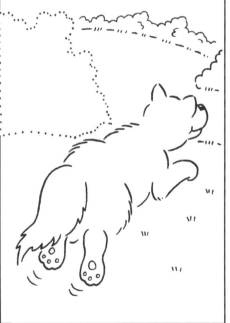

E But the fox was frightened and ran back to the fields.

F There, curled up in the corner, was a fox!

1 ☐ **2** ☐ **3** ☐   **4** ☐ **5** ☐ **6** ☐

Good spells!

Wanda Witch has written the ingredients for her favorite spells.
Write them in your neatest handwriting, but be sure to correct her spelling!

whing of bat

skin of snaike

whiska of kitten

shoo of horse

tode slime

snaill shell

wool of lam

green custerd

milk of gote

mane of lyon

tale of rat

egg of oztrich

peacock fether

toe nales

webb of spyder

tooth of dragen

Fairy-tale postcards

Use your imagination to finish writing these fairy-tale postcards.
The first one has been done for you.

Dear Snow White,

How are you? The seven of us miss you very much. Grumpy has been really grumpy and Happy has been really sad!
Write back to us soon.

Lots of love,

The Seven Dwarfs

Snow White

The Enchanted castle

High Mountains

Magical Kingdom

00647

Dear Tom Thumb,

_____
_____
_____
_____
_____
_____
_____

Master Tom Thumb

_____
_____
_____

Hi Grandma,

_____
_____
_____
_____

Love,
Little Red Riding Hood

Grandma

_____
_____
_____

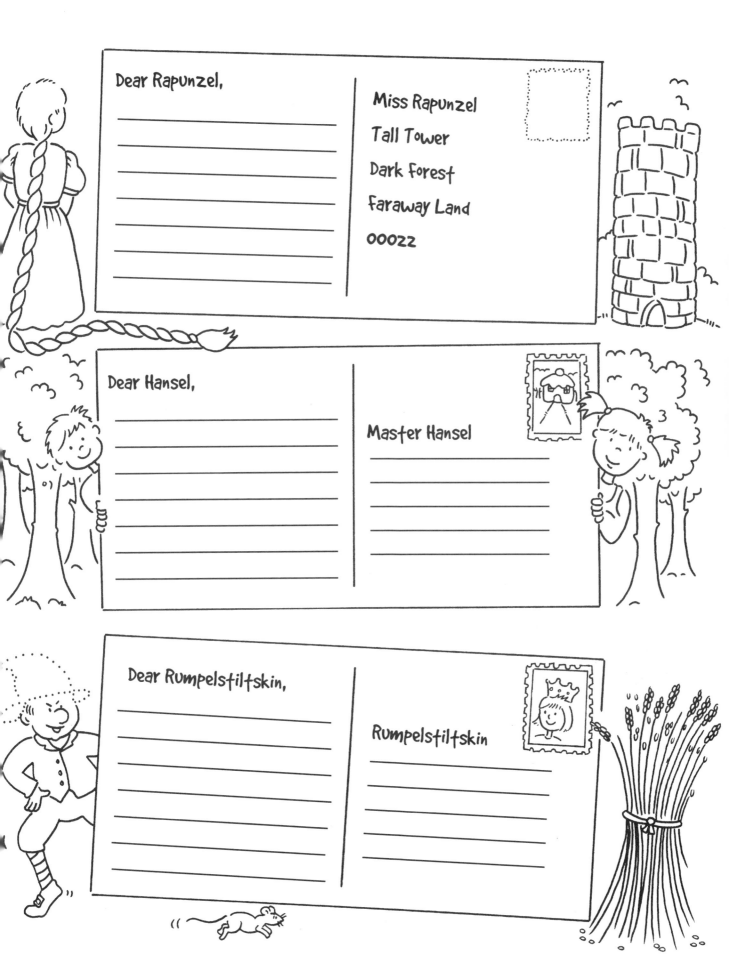

Dear Rapunzel,
_____
_____
_____
_____
_____
_____

Miss Rapunzel
Tall Tower
Dark Forest
Faraway Land
OOO2Z

Dear Hansel,
_____
_____
_____
_____
_____
_____

Master Hansel
_____
_____
_____

Dear Rumpelstiltskin,
_____
_____
_____
_____
_____

Rumpelstiltskin
_____
_____
_____

Magic symbols

The Great Alphonso has made the punctuation magically disappear from these sentences. Rewrite the sentences, punctuating them correctly. You will need the following:

?	5 question marks	A	23 capital letters
!	3 exclamation marks	,	6 commas
"	18 quotation marks	.	14 periods

can you go to the store for me his mother asked

----

lizzie john and anna took the dog for a walk

----

it was fantastic he yelled

----

why does this always happen to me laughed jasmine

----

the twins told their brother they were going to be late

----

are you traveling on this train patrick asked

----

watch out he shouted

----

she turned the corner and ran into the house

----

why do I have to do this gwen asked

----

would she get there on time

----

they grabbed their bags coats and books and ran out the door

----

maria said i can't wait to go on vacation

----

it was not long before they heard the sound again

----

look at the snow cried mark

----

frank turned and said you have to move your car

Up, up, and away

Write a story to go with these pictures.
The first one has been done for you.

1. Colin and Claire have always wanted to take a balloon ride.

2. _____

3. _____

4. _____

5. _____

6. _____

8.

9.

11.

12.

Lights, camera, action!

Find the stickers and put them in place. There are two different storylines hidden in this passage. Direct the story by circling the words you want to use. The pictures are clues.

Washington Smith spotted the **emerald/fish** he had been searching for, shining in the **eyes/lid** of a huge **freezer/statue**. He gently eased himself through the **tunnel/aisle** and reached down into the **freezer/statue**. With a steady hand, he carefully lifted the **emerald/fish** out and placed it in his empty **shopping cart/pocket**. He began to hear a **squeaking/rumbling** sound. "Aargh!" he screamed, as a runaway **boulder/shopping cart** came hurtling down the **tunnel/aisle** toward him. As he fell to the floor, the **fish/emerald** slipped from his grasp and flew through the air, falling into the **lair/lap** of the angry **cashier/dragon**.

Chewy snack bars

Look at the pictures of these children making snack bars.
Write the instructions to go with them.
The first one has been done for you.

1. Grease a shallow cake pan

with a little butter.

2. _____

_____

3. _____

_____

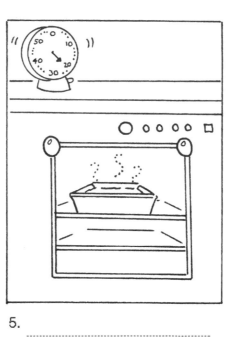

4. _____

_____

5. _____

_____

6. _____

_____

Vinnie the Vowel Muncher

Vinnie the Vowel Muncher has munched some of the vowels in this paragraph.
Add the missing vowels.

V_nni_ w_s v_ry h_ngry _nd
m_nched s_me _f th_ v_wels
in th_s pi_ce of writ_ng. He
nev_r w_nt to sch_ol _nd d_es
not kn_w h_w m_ny vow_ls
ther_ ar_ in the alphabet.
V_wels jo_n th_ oth_r l_tters
t_geth_r. Th_re ar_ v_ry f_w
w_rds that do n_t h_ve _t
le_st on_ vow_l. Lo_k _t th_
w_y th_ vow_ls beh_ve wh_n
yo_ re_d. The_r so_nds c_n
ch_nge fr_m w_rd t_ w_rd.

How the tortoise got its shell

Read the story and answer the questions below.

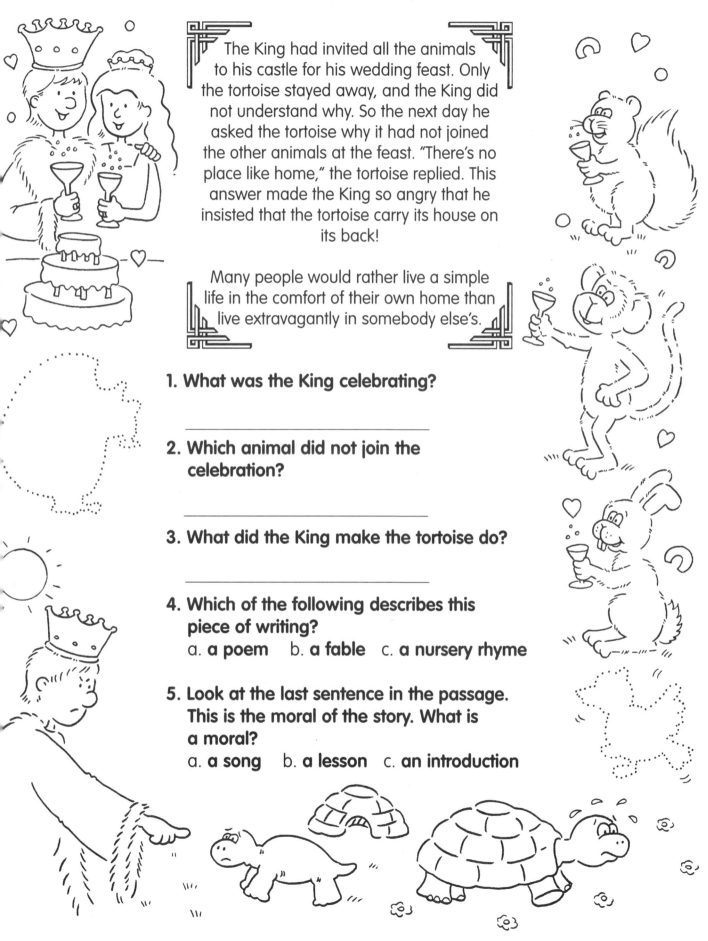

The King had invited all the animals to his castle for his wedding feast. Only the tortoise stayed away, and the King did not understand why. So the next day he asked the tortoise why it had not joined the other animals at the feast. "There's no place like home," the tortoise replied. This answer made the King so angry that he insisted that the tortoise carry its house on its back!

Many people would rather live a simple life in the comfort of their own home than live extravagantly in somebody else's.

1. What was the King celebrating?

_____

2. Which animal did not join the celebration?

_____

3. What did the King make the tortoise do?

_____

4. Which of the following describes this piece of writing?
   a. **a poem**   b. **a fable**   c. **a nursery rhyme**

5. Look at the last sentence in the passage. This is the moral of the story. What is a moral?
   a. **a song**   b. **a lesson**   c. **an introduction**

Play poster

Look at the information in the box. Write it in the correct order on the poster.

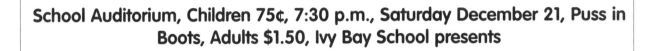

School Auditorium, Children 75¢, 7:30 p.m., Saturday December 21, Puss in Boots, Adults $1.50, Ivy Bay School presents

The Grand Old Duke of York

Put the rhyme in the correct order by numbering the boxes from 1 to 4.

He marched them up to the
top of the hill,
And he marched them down again.

And when they were up they were up,
And when they were down,
they were down,

And when they were only halfway up,
They were neither up nor down.

Oh, the grand old Duke of York,
He had ten thousand men;

Down under wordsearch

Look in the wordsearch grid for six things you might find in Australia.
You will find them by reading across or down.
Circle the words as you find them.

K	A	N	G	A	R	O	O	D	U
B	O	S	E	V	L	X	N	U	B
O	X	M	I	F	Z	E	E	N	W
O	D	E	P	H	K	C	H	O	A
M	O	W	O	M	B	A	T	I	L
E	L	A	S	I	D	N	Z	R	L
R	O	D	S	O	K	O	A	L	A
A	I	T	U	N	Q	R	C	H	B
N	E	E	M	C	F	D	Q	R	Y
G	A	W	S	U	V	X	N	L	T

Alphabet names

Think of a name for a boy or girl that begins
with each letter of the alphabet.

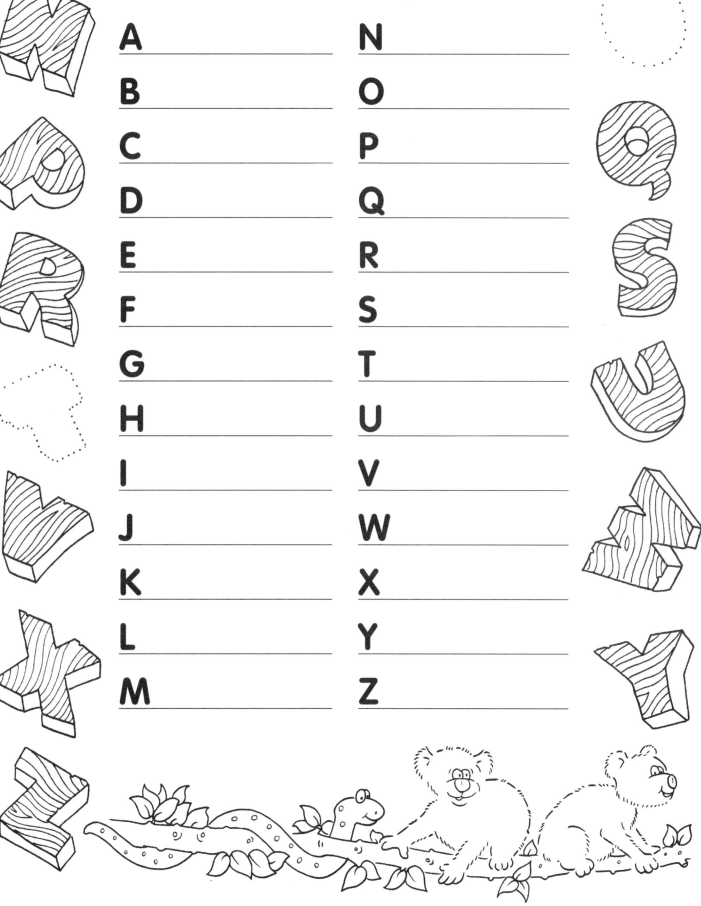

A _____

B _____

C _____

D _____

E _____

F _____

G _____

H _____

I _____

J _____

K _____

L _____

M _____

N _____

O _____

P _____

Q _____

R _____

S _____

T _____

U _____

V _____

W _____

X _____

Y _____

Z _____

On the shelf

Encyclopedias are information books that are usually arranged in alphabetical order. Look at these encyclopedias and write which book you would look in for the subjects below. The first one has been done for you.

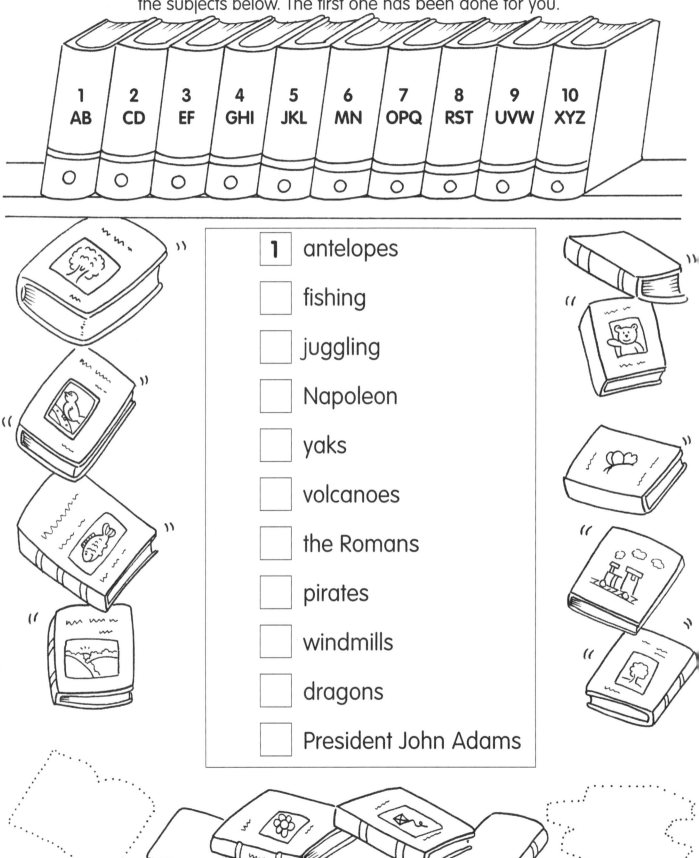

Books on shelf:
1 AB 2 CD 3 EF 4 GHI 5 JKL 6 MN 7 OPQ 8 RST 9 UVW 10 XYZ

1	antelopes
	fishing
	juggling
	Napoleon
	yaks
	volcanoes
	the Romans
	pirates
	windmills
	dragons
	President John Adams

Tense time

The **past** tense tells us what has already happened. The **present** tense tells us about something that is happening. The **future** tense tells us about something that is going to happen. In which tense are these sentences written?

1. Farmer Green grows potatoes in his fields.

past/present/future

2. Carl the crow ate all the seeds.

past/present/future

3. When we get a scarecrow it will help scare the birds.

past/present/future

4. There are lots of rabbits in the fields.

past/present/future

5. The rabbits dug lots of burrows.

past/present/future

6. The gate to the field is closed.

past/present/future

7. Farmer Green will plant more seeds in the morning.

past/present/future

8. Farmer Green's tractor is red.

past/present/future

What's it all about?

Look at the titles of these books. The contents and chapter headings are written next to each one. Look at the questions in the box. Write your answers on the lines.

How Things Work

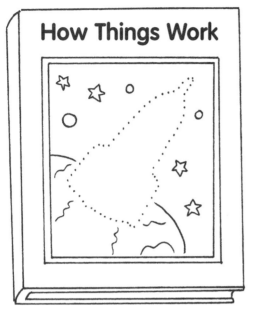

Contents
Safety First
Wheels at Work
Rocket Power
Electrifying Activity
Glossary and Index

Chapters
Bad News
Abandoned
Discovery at the Field
The Search
Unwilling Hunter
Captured
A Memory

The Midnight Fox

The Complete Book of Gardening

Contents
Designing your Garden
The Fruit and Vegetable Garden
Decorative Garden Plants
Gardening Techniques
Glossary and Index

A Journey Through Time

Contents

Mountains and Valleys

Contents

1. Which book is about history? . . . .

2. Which book is about science? . . . .

3. Which book tells you how to grow tomatoes? . . . .

4. Which book is fiction? . . . .

5. All the other books are nonfiction. What do they have in common? . . . . .

. . . .

. . . .

Jock Jackdaw's punctuation

Mischievous Jock Jackdaw has stolen some of the punctuation and capital letters from this story. Can you see what is missing?

The Magic Porridge Pot

Once upon a time there was a little girl who lived with her mother. they were very poor and had nothing to eat One day the girl met an old woman who gave her a little pot. All she had to say was, "cook, little pot, cook, and the pot would cook good, sweet porridge. to make it stop cooking she just had to say "Stop, little pot, stop"

one day when the girl went for a walk, the mother felt hungry and asked the pot to cook But she did not know how to stop it and soon the porridge began to cover the kitchen and then the house it was not long before all the houses in the street were full of porridge

Just as the porridge was reaching the last house in town, the little girl came home and said, Stop, little pot, stop from that day on anyone who wanted to come back to the town had to eat their way through the porridge.

Rewrite the story in your neatest handwriting and add
the punctuation and capital letters.

_____

_____

_____

_____

_____

_____

_____

_____

_____

_____

_____

_____

_____

_____

_____

_____

Barnyard crossword

Find the stickers and put them in place. The pictures are clues to these barnyard things. Follow the numbers across and down and complete the crossword.

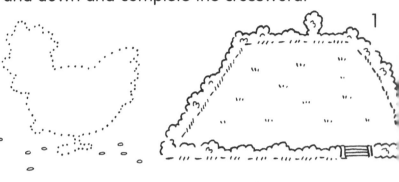

Rhyming balloons

Find the words that rhyme and color the balloons the same color.

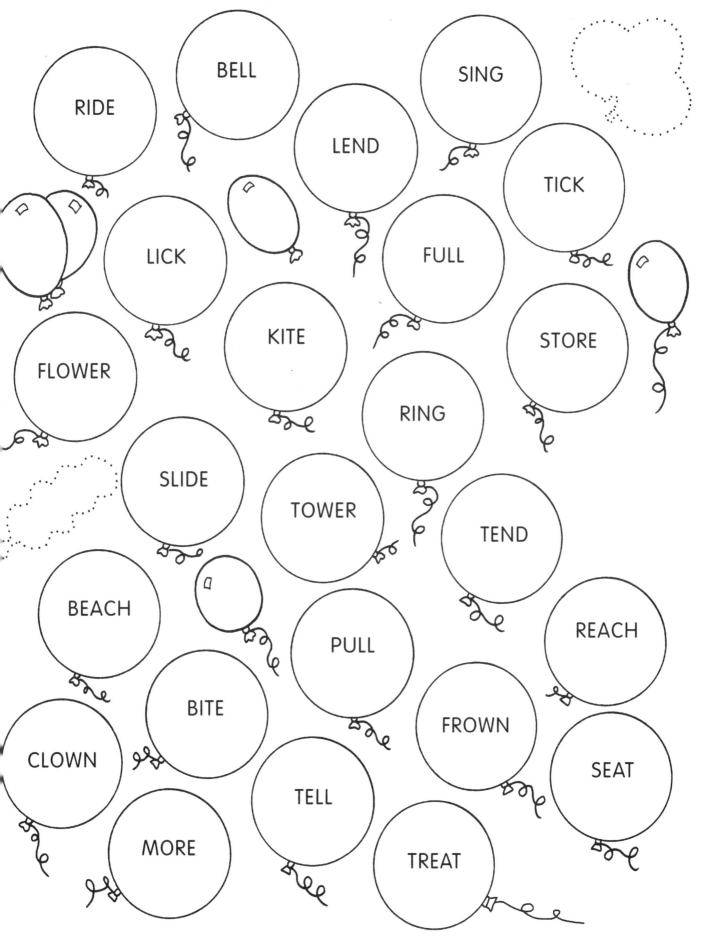

The Three Billy Goats Gruff

Read this story, then answer the questions on the next page.

Once there were three billy goats called Gruff. They lived in the mountains, searching for the fresh, green grass they loved to eat. On the other side of a river was the freshest, greenest grass they had ever seen. The goats trotted toward the river until they came to a bridge.

"The bridge may not be very strong," said the smallest goat. "I will go first to make sure it is safe."

Under the bridge there lived a wicked old troll. When the smallest goat's hooves went trip, trap on the wooden planks, the troll peeked over the edge of the bridge.

"Who's that trip-trapping across my bridge? I'm a troll and I'm going to eat you for my dinner!" he roared.
But the goat replied, "I'm the smallest billy goat Gruff. My brother will be tastier than me." So the troll let the smallest goat go.

Next the middle-sized goat began to cross the bridge. When he was in the middle, the wicked old troll popped up again.

"Who's that trip-trapping across my bridge?" he roared.
"I'll eat you up!"
But the middle-sized goat replied, "Wait for my brother. He is much bigger!" So the greedy troll let the middle-sized goat go.

The biggest goat had seen everything that had happened and smiled to himself. His big hooves went trip, trap on the wooden planks. This time the troll jumped out and stood on the bridge.

"Who's that trip-trapping on my bridge?" he shouted. "Dinner at last!"

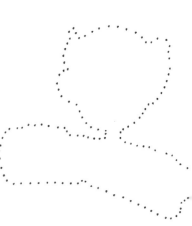

"I'm the biggest billy goat Gruff," came the reply. He lowered his horns and CHARGED!

With a great roar, the troll flew into the air and into the river below. The water carried him away, never to be seen again, and the billy goats Gruff lived happily ever after.

1. How many goats were there?

----

2. Where did the goats live?

----

3. Which two words are used to describe the grass on the other side of the river?

----

4. What sound did the goats' hooves make when they crossed the bridge?

----

5. Find two words that describe the troll.

----

6. Why did the troll let the smallest billy goat Gruff cross the bridge?

----

7. 'He lowered his horns and CHARGED!' Why is the word CHARGED written in capital letters?

----

8. Which of the following describes this type of writing?

a. **a diary**   b. **a nursery rhyme**   c. **a fairy tale**

Finish the poem!

Think of the best rhyming words to complete this poem.

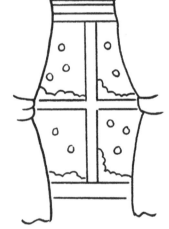

I like spring, when the lambs come to play,
During the months of March, April, and _ _ _ .

I think hot summer days are grand!
I go to the beach and dig in the _ _ _ _ .

I like fall, when the winds blow free,
shaking the leaves from every _ _ _ _ _ .

I love winter, when there's a snowstorm, And
I'm inside with Pup, all snug and _ _ _ _ _ .

Answers

In town

MOVIE THEATER STAR WARS BUTCHER CHURCH PARK DOWNTOWN BAKERY GREENGROCER EAST STREET FISH STORE RESTAURANT

A sleepy surprise

1C 2D 3B 4F 5A 6E

Good spells

wing of bat, skin of snake, whisker of kitten, shoe of horse, toad slime, snail shell, wool of lamb, green custard, milk of goat, mane of lion, tail of rat, egg of ostrich, peacock feather, toe nails, web of spider, tooth of dragon

Magic symbols

"Can you go to the store for me?" his mother asked.

Lizzie, John, and Anna took the dog for a walk.

"It was fantastic!" he yelled.

"Why does this always happen to me?" laughed Jasmine.

The twins told their brother they were going to be late.

"Are you traveling on this train?" Patrick asked.

"Watch out!" he shouted.

She turned the corner and ran into the house.

"Why do I have to do this?" Gwen asked.

Would she get there on time?

They grabbed their bags, coats, and books and ran out the door.

Maria said, "I can't wait to go on vacation."

It was not long before they heard the sound again.

"Look at the snow!" cried Mark.

Frank turned and said, "You have to move your car."

Vinnie the Vowel Muncher

Vinnie was very hungry and munched some of the vowels in this piece of writing. He never went to school and does not know how many vowels there are in the alphabet. Vowels join the other letters together. There are very few words that do not have at least one vowel. Look at the way the vowels behave when you read. Their sounds can change from word to word.

How the tortoise got its shell

1. The King was celebrating his wedding.
2. The tortoise did not join the celebration.
3. The King made the tortoise carry its house on its back.
4. **b.** a fable
5. **b.** a lesson

The Grand Old Duke of York

1. Oh, the grand old Duke of York,
   He had ten thousand men;
2. He marched them up to the top of the hill,
   And he marched them down again.
3. And when they were up they were up,
   And when they were down, they were down,
4. And when they were only halfway up,
   They were neither up nor down.

Down under wordsearch

On the shelf

3–fishing, 5–juggling, 6–Napoleon
10–yaks, 9–volcanoes, 8–the Romans
7–pirates, 9–windmills, 2–dragons
1–President John Adams ("Adams" not "President" or "John"!)

Tense time

1. present 2. past 3. future 4. present
5. past 6. present 7. future 8. present

What's it all about?

1. A Journey Through Time
2. How Things Work
3. The Complete Book of Gardening
4. The Midnight Fox
5. All of the other books are factual and informative. They also have a glossary and/or an index.

Jock Jackdaw's punctuation
The Magic Porridge Pot

Once upon a time there was a little girl who lived with her mother. They were very poor and had nothing to eat. One day the girl met an old woman who gave her a little pot. All she had to say was, "Cook, little pot, cook," and the pot would cook good, sweet porridge. To make it stop cooking she just had to say "Stop, little pot, stop."

One day when the girl went for a walk, the mother felt hungry and asked the pot to cook. But she did not know how to stop it, and soon the porridge began to cover the kitchen and then the house. It was not long before all the houses in the street were full of porridge.

Just as the porridge was reaching the last house in town, the little girl came home and said, "Stop, little pot, stop. "From that day on, anyone who wanted to come back to the town had to eat their way through the porridge.

Barnyard crossword

```
              ²f        ¹f
    ²f a r m ⁴h o u s e  i
    r        a         l
    m        y         d
    e    ⁵c
  ⁶r o o s ⁷t e r
      w    r
        ⁸b a r n
           c
           t
  ⁹h o r s e
           r
```

Rhyming balloons

RIDE–SLIDE, BELL–TELL, LEND–TEND
SING–RING, TICK–LICK, FULL–PULL
STORE–MORE, KITE–BITE, FLOWER–TOWER
REACH–BEACH, FROWN–CLOWN, SEAT–TREAT

The Three Billy Goats Gruff

1. There were three goats.
2. They lived in the mountains.
3. The words "fresh" and "green" are used to describe the grass.
4. The goats' hooves made a "trip-trapping" sound on the bridge.
5. There are three words that are used to describe the troll: "wicked", "old", and "greedy".
6. The troll was greedy and waited for the smallest goat's bigger brother to cross the bridge, because there would be more for him to eat.
7. "CHARGED" is written in capital letters to make the word stand out and to give more emphasis.
8. **c.** a fairy tale

Finish the poem!

I like spring, when the lambs come to play,
During the months of March, April, and **May**.

I think hot summer days are grand!
I go to the beach and dig in the **sand**.

I like fall, when the winds blow free,
shaking the leaves from every **tree**.

I love winter, when there's a snowstorm,
And I'm inside with Pup, all snug and **warm**.

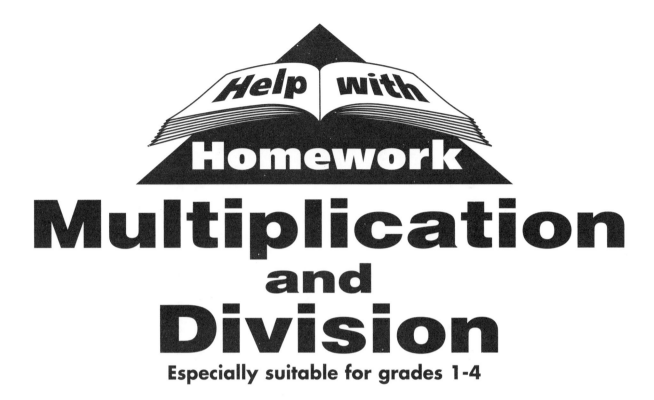

Multiplication and Division

Especially suitable for grades 1-4

Multiplication tables

Learn the multiplication tables and remember them.

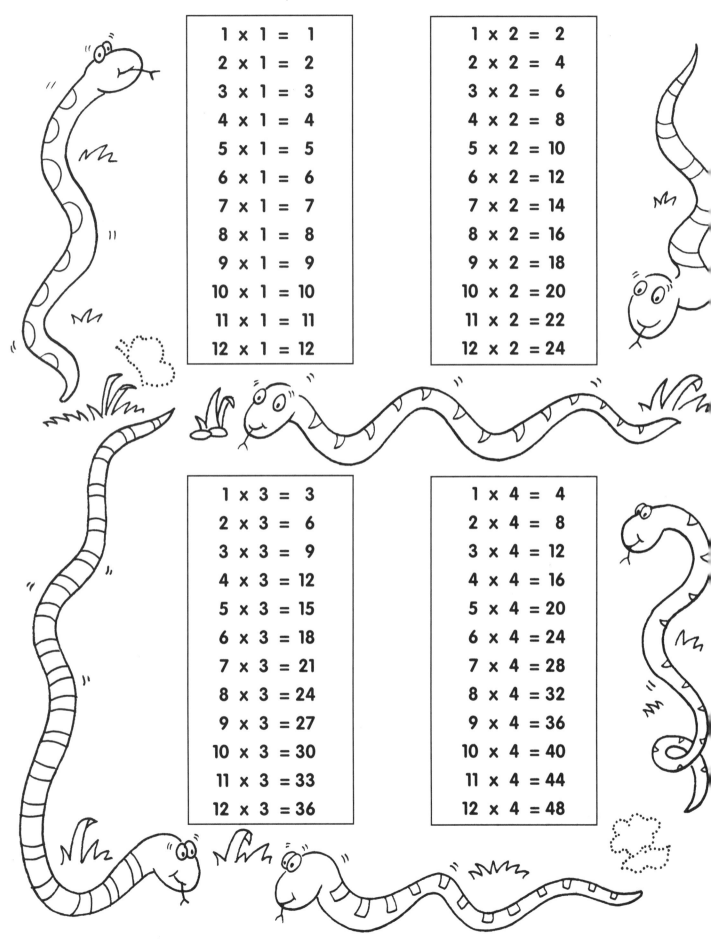

1 x 1 = 1		1 x 2 = 2
2 x 1 = 2		2 x 2 = 4
3 x 1 = 3		3 x 2 = 6
4 x 1 = 4		4 x 2 = 8
5 x 1 = 5		5 x 2 = 10
6 x 1 = 6		6 x 2 = 12
7 x 1 = 7		7 x 2 = 14
8 x 1 = 8		8 x 2 = 16
9 x 1 = 9		9 x 2 = 18
10 x 1 = 10		10 x 2 = 20
11 x 1 = 11		11 x 2 = 22
12 x 1 = 12		12 x 2 = 24

1 x 3 = 3		1 x 4 = 4
2 x 3 = 6		2 x 4 = 8
3 x 3 = 9		3 x 4 = 12
4 x 3 = 12		4 x 4 = 16
5 x 3 = 15		5 x 4 = 20
6 x 3 = 18		6 x 4 = 24
7 x 3 = 21		7 x 4 = 28
8 x 3 = 24		8 x 4 = 32
9 x 3 = 27		9 x 4 = 36
10 x 3 = 30		10 x 4 = 40
11 x 3 = 33		11 x 4 = 44
12 x 3 = 36		12 x 4 = 48

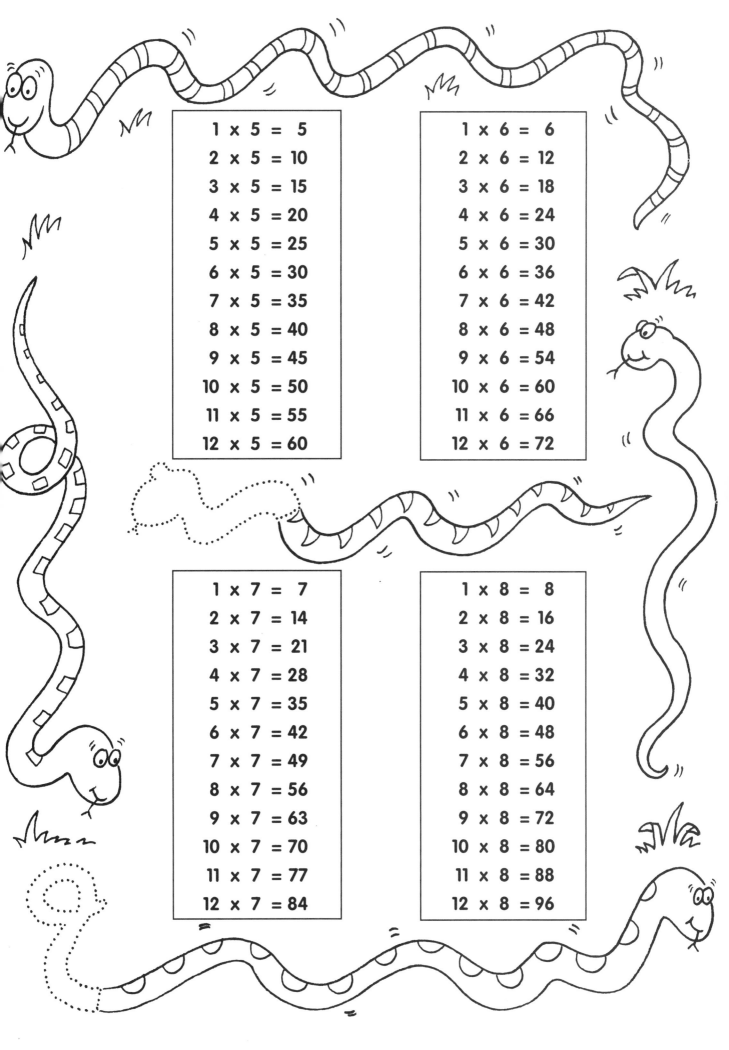

1 x 5 = 5		1 x 6 = 6
2 x 5 = 10		2 x 6 = 12
3 x 5 = 15		3 x 6 = 18
4 x 5 = 20		4 x 6 = 24
5 x 5 = 25		5 x 6 = 30
6 x 5 = 30		6 x 6 = 36
7 x 5 = 35		7 x 6 = 42
8 x 5 = 40		8 x 6 = 48
9 x 5 = 45		9 x 6 = 54
10 x 5 = 50		10 x 6 = 60
11 x 5 = 55		11 x 6 = 66
12 x 5 = 60		12 x 6 = 72

1 x 7 = 7		1 x 8 = 8
2 x 7 = 14		2 x 8 = 16
3 x 7 = 21		3 x 8 = 24
4 x 7 = 28		4 x 8 = 32
5 x 7 = 35		5 x 8 = 40
6 x 7 = 42		6 x 8 = 48
7 x 7 = 49		7 x 8 = 56
8 x 7 = 56		8 x 8 = 64
9 x 7 = 63		9 x 8 = 72
10 x 7 = 70		10 x 8 = 80
11 x 7 = 77		11 x 8 = 88
12 x 7 = 84		12 x 8 = 96

1 x 9 = 9		1 x 10 = 10
2 x 9 = 18		2 x 10 = 20
3 x 9 = 27		3 x 10 = 30
4 x 9 = 36		4 x 10 = 40
5 x 9 = 45		5 x 10 = 50
6 x 9 = 54		6 x 10 = 60
7 x 9 = 63		7 x 10 = 70
8 x 9 = 72		8 x 10 = 80
9 x 9 = 81		9 x 10 = 90
10 x 9 = 90		10 x 10 = 100
11 x 9 = 99		11 x 10 = 110
12 x 9 = 108		12 x 10 = 120

1 x 11 = 11		1 x 12 = 12
2 x 11 = 22		2 x 12 = 24
3 x 11 = 33		3 x 12 = 36
4 x 11 = 44		4 x 12 = 48
5 x 11 = 55		5 x 12 = 60
6 x 11 = 66		6 x 12 = 72
7 x 11 = 77		7 x 12 = 84
8 x 11 = 88		8 x 12 = 96
9 x 11 = 99		9 x 12 = 108
10 x 11 = 110		10 x 12 = 120
11 x 11 = 121		11 x 12 = 132
12 x 11 = 132		12 x 12 = 144

Math pails

Do the multiplication and write the answers on the pails.

3 × 2 =

5 × 5 =

9 × 6 =

Multiplication problems

Do the multiplication and write the answers on the rocks.

3 x 8 =

5 x 6 =

7 x 2 =

Missing numbers

Complete the multiplication problems.

$2 \times \boxed{} = 4$

$\boxed{} \times 5 = 15$

$7 \times \boxed{} = 14$

$3 \times 3 = \boxed{}$

$\boxed{} \times 5 = 30$

$9 \times \boxed{} = 18$

$4 \times 5 = \boxed{}$

$\boxed{} \times 3 = 3$

$4 \times 4 = \boxed{}$

$7 \times \boxed{} = 56$

$\boxed{} \times 4 = 8$

$11 \times 3 = \boxed{}$

$9 \times \boxed{} = 45$

$6 \times \boxed{} = 36$

$8 \times 3 = \boxed{}$

$\boxed{} \times 7 = 28$

12 × 5 = ☐

10 × ☐ = 30

4 × 3 = ☐

☐ × 11 = 11

8 × ☐ = 40

9 × 3 = ☐

8 × ☐ = 72

12 × 12 = ☐

11 × 10 = ☐

6 × ☐ = 48

☐ × 4 = 24

7 × 9 = ☐

2 × ☐ = 4

12 × 8 = ☐

9 × 9 = ☐

3 × ☐ = 21

Magical numbers

The children are holding the answers to the problems on the cooking pots.
Draw a line to join each child to the correct pot.

3 x 3

4 x 6

10 x 9

Match the answers

Do the multiplication on the spaceships. Look at the answers, then draw a line to connect each alien to the correct spaceship.

7 x 8 =

9 x 9 =

3 x 3 =

56

81

9

Missing bees

Draw more bees to complete the problems.

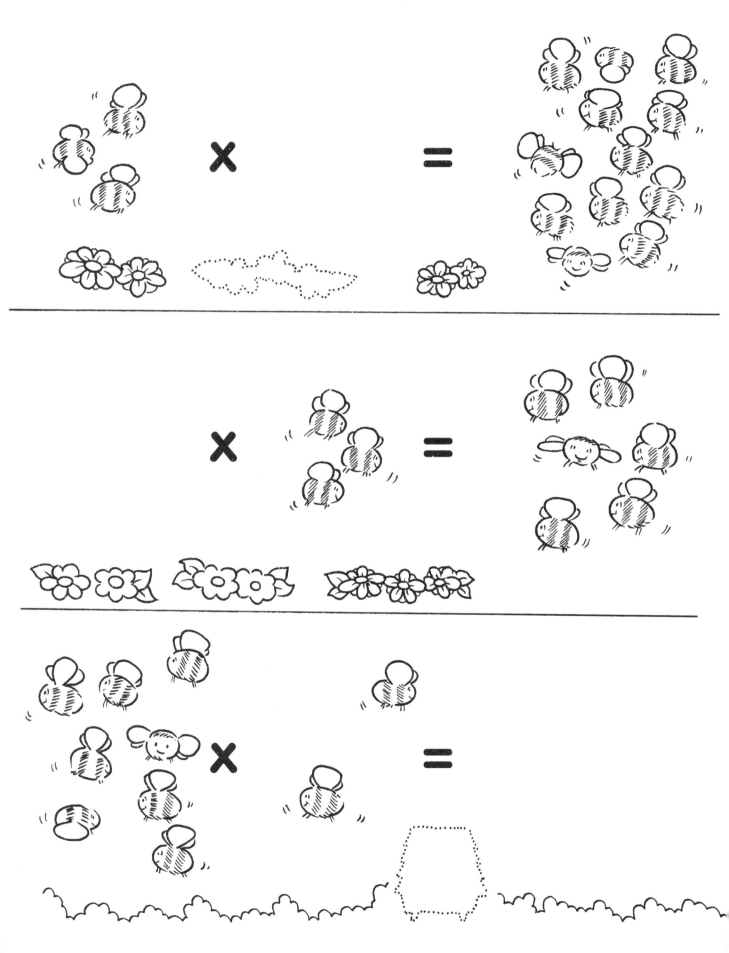

Flower math

Count the petals and write the number in the center of each flower,
then do the multiplication. Draw the missing petals on the last flower in each row.
Look at the example to help you.

Example:

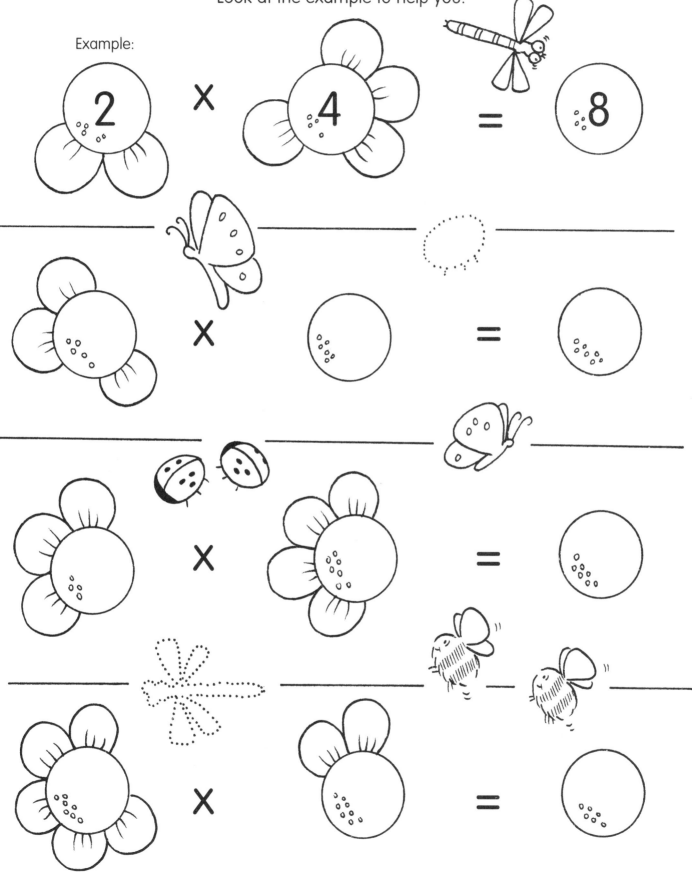

Number puzzles

Complete the problems in the grids by filling in the missing numbers.

Number crossword

Do the multiplication. Following the letters across and down, write the answers as words in the crossword grid.

a. $3 \times 4 = \boxed{}$

b. $2 \times 1 = \boxed{}$

→ c. $2 \times 7 = \boxed{}$

↓ c. $5 \times 10 = \boxed{}$

d. $3 \times 3 = \boxed{}$

e. $1 \times 11 = \boxed{}$

f. $7 \times 10 = \boxed{}$

g. $10 \times 1 = \boxed{}$

Multiplication test

Do the multiplication and write the answers in the boxes.
Check your answers by looking back at the multiplication tables.

2 x 2 = ☐

4 x 5 = ☐

8 x 8 = ☐

1 x 3 = ☐

5 x 8 = ☐

6 x 7 = ☐

11 x 2 = ☐

10 x 10 = ☐

6 x 9 = ☐

3 x 12 = ☐

2 x 8 = ☐

7 x 6 = ☐

5 x 5 = ☐

7 × 12 = ☐

3 × 9 = ☐

4 × 4 = ☐

5 × 6 = ☐

4 × 7 = ☐

9 × 6 = ☐

11 × 11 = ☐

8 × 4 = ☐

12 × 6 = ☐

1 × 9 = ☐

3 × 3 = ☐

6 × 6 = ☐

8 × 3 = ☐

Division tables

Learn the division tables and remember them.

1 ÷ 1 = 1	2 ÷ 2 = 1
2 ÷ 1 = 2	4 ÷ 2 = 2
3 ÷ 1 = 3	6 ÷ 2 = 3
4 ÷ 1 = 4	8 ÷ 2 = 4
5 ÷ 1 = 5	10 ÷ 2 = 5
6 ÷ 1 = 6	12 ÷ 2 = 6
7 ÷ 1 = 7	14 ÷ 2 = 7
8 ÷ 1 = 8	16 ÷ 2 = 8
9 ÷ 1 = 9	18 ÷ 2 = 9
10 ÷ 1 = 10	20 ÷ 2 = 10
11 ÷ 1 = 11	22 ÷ 2 = 11
12 ÷ 1 = 12	24 ÷ 2 = 12

3 ÷ 3 = 1	4 ÷ 4 = 1
6 ÷ 3 = 2	8 ÷ 4 = 2
9 ÷ 3 = 3	12 ÷ 4 = 3
12 ÷ 3 = 4	16 ÷ 4 = 4
15 ÷ 3 = 5	20 ÷ 4 = 5
18 ÷ 3 = 6	24 ÷ 4 = 6
21 ÷ 3 = 7	28 ÷ 4 = 7
24 ÷ 3 = 8	32 ÷ 4 = 8
27 ÷ 3 = 9	36 ÷ 4 = 9
30 ÷ 3 = 10	40 ÷ 4 = 10
33 ÷ 3 = 11	44 ÷ 4 = 11
36 ÷ 3 = 12	48 ÷ 4 = 12

5	÷	5	=	1
10	÷	5	=	2
15	÷	5	=	3
20	÷	5	=	4
25	÷	5	=	5
30	÷	5	=	6
35	÷	5	=	7
40	÷	5	=	8
45	÷	5	=	9
50	÷	5	=	10
55	÷	5	=	11
60	÷	5	=	12

$5 \div 5 = 1$
$10 \div 5 = 2$
$15 \div 5 = 3$
$20 \div 5 = 4$
$25 \div 5 = 5$
$30 \div 5 = 6$
$35 \div 5 = 7$
$40 \div 5 = 8$
$45 \div 5 = 9$
$50 \div 5 = 10$
$55 \div 5 = 11$
$60 \div 5 = 12$

$6 \div 6 = 1$
$12 \div 6 = 2$
$18 \div 6 = 3$
$24 \div 6 = 4$
$30 \div 6 = 5$
$36 \div 6 = 6$
$42 \div 6 = 7$
$48 \div 6 = 8$
$54 \div 6 = 9$
$60 \div 6 = 10$
$66 \div 6 = 11$
$72 \div 6 = 12$

$7 \div 7 = 1$
$14 \div 7 = 2$
$21 \div 7 = 3$
$28 \div 7 = 4$
$35 \div 7 = 5$
$42 \div 7 = 6$
$49 \div 7 = 7$
$56 \div 7 = 8$
$63 \div 7 = 9$
$70 \div 7 = 10$
$77 \div 7 = 11$
$84 \div 7 = 12$

$8 \div 8 = 1$
$16 \div 8 = 2$
$24 \div 8 = 3$
$32 \div 8 = 4$
$40 \div 8 = 5$
$48 \div 8 = 6$
$56 \div 8 = 7$
$64 \div 8 = 8$
$72 \div 8 = 9$
$80 \div 8 = 10$
$88 \div 8 = 11$
$96 \div 8 = 12$

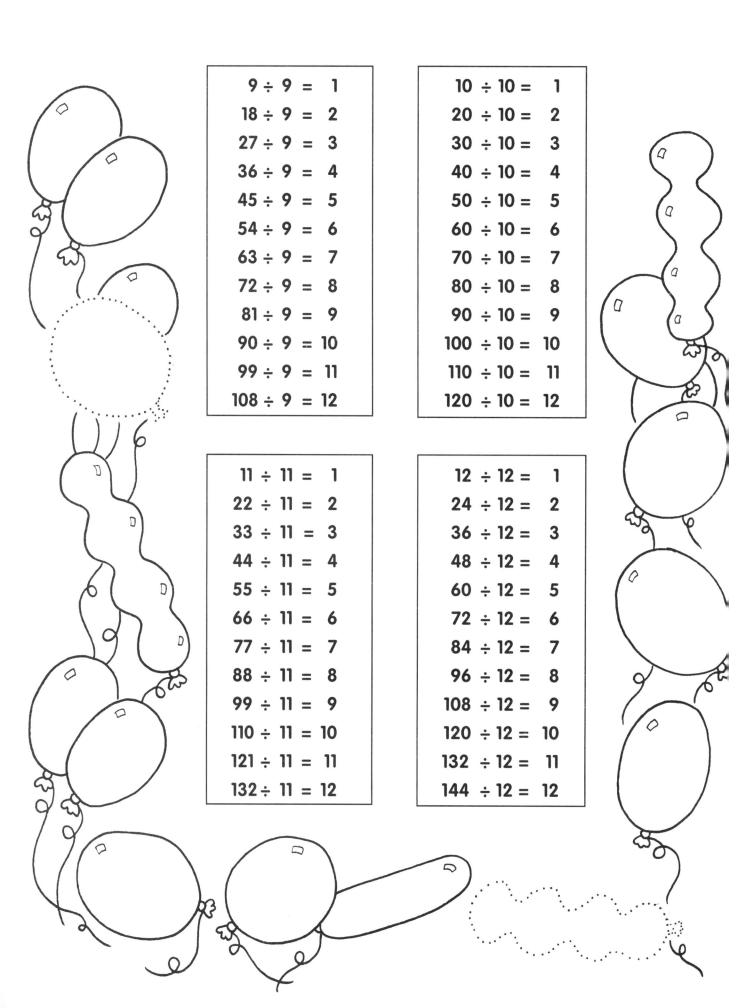

9 ÷ 9 =	1	10 ÷ 10 =	1
18 ÷ 9 =	2	20 ÷ 10 =	2
27 ÷ 9 =	3	30 ÷ 10 =	3
36 ÷ 9 =	4	40 ÷ 10 =	4
45 ÷ 9 =	5	50 ÷ 10 =	5
54 ÷ 9 =	6	60 ÷ 10 =	6
63 ÷ 9 =	7	70 ÷ 10 =	7
72 ÷ 9 =	8	80 ÷ 10 =	8
81 ÷ 9 =	9	90 ÷ 10 =	9
90 ÷ 9 =	10	100 ÷ 10 =	10
99 ÷ 9 =	11	110 ÷ 10 =	11
108 ÷ 9 =	12	120 ÷ 10 =	12

11 ÷ 11 =	1	12 ÷ 12 =	1
22 ÷ 11 =	2	24 ÷ 12 =	2
33 ÷ 11 =	3	36 ÷ 12 =	3
44 ÷ 11 =	4	48 ÷ 12 =	4
55 ÷ 11 =	5	60 ÷ 12 =	5
66 ÷ 11 =	6	72 ÷ 12 =	6
77 ÷ 11 =	7	84 ÷ 12 =	7
88 ÷ 11 =	8	96 ÷ 12 =	8
99 ÷ 11 =	9	108 ÷ 12 =	9
110 ÷ 11 =	10	120 ÷ 12 =	10
121 ÷ 11 =	11	132 ÷ 12 =	11
132 ÷ 11 =	12	144 ÷ 12 =	12

Groups

Draw circles around the following animals to divide them into groups.

GROUPS OF 2

GROUPS OF 4

GROUPS OF 3

Juggling math

Complete the problems by filling in the missing numbers.

$6 \div 3 = \square$

$\square \div 2 = 8$

$\square \div 7 = 6$

$24 \div \square = 6$

$27 \div 3 = \square$

$30 \div 5 = \square$

$9 \div \square = 9$

$\square \div 9 = 7$

Missing numbers

Complete the problems.

4 ÷ ☐ = 1

☐ ÷ 4 = 2

21 ÷ ☐ = 3

54 ÷ 6 = ☐

☐ ÷ 6 = 6

63 ÷ ☐ = 7

49 ÷ 7 = ☐

☐ ÷ 9 = 11

12 ÷ 6 = ☐

36 ÷ ☐ = 4

☐ ÷ 9 = 1

56 ÷ 7 = ☐

42 ÷ ☐ = 6

18 ÷ ☐ = 3

20 ÷ 4 = ☐

☐ ÷ 7 = 4

$24 \div \boxed{} = 4$

$\boxed{} \div 9 = 2$

$70 \div \boxed{} = 10$

$99 \div 9 = \boxed{}$

$\boxed{} \div 6 = 8$

$27 \div \boxed{} = 3$

$32 \div 4 = \boxed{}$

$\boxed{} \div 9 = 5$

$30 \div 6 = \boxed{}$

$10 \div \boxed{} = 2$

$\boxed{} \div 8 = 9$

$40 \div 5 = \boxed{}$

$90 \div \boxed{} = 9$

$56 \div \boxed{} = 7$

$6 \div 3 = \boxed{}$

$\boxed{} \div 8 = 3$

Butterfly math

Draw more butterflies to complete the problems.

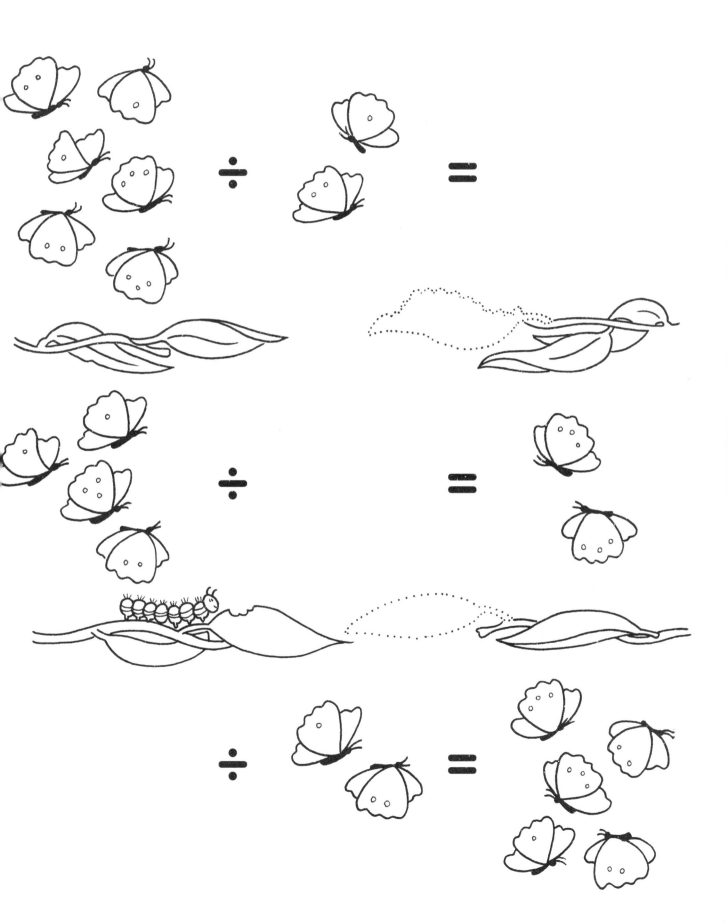

Star math

Do the division in the stars and write the answers in the boxes.

$81 \div 9$

$35 \div 5$

$49 \div 7$

$12 \div 6$

$20 \div 5$

$3 \div 3$

$32 \div 4$

$55 \div 11$

Solve these problems

Share 16 books equally between 4 children.
How many books each?

Share 7 ice cream cones equally between 3 children. How many cones each?
How many left over?

Share 8 carrots equally between 2 rabbits.
How many carrots each?

Share 14 bananas equally between 7 monkeys.
How many bananas each?

Share 9 peanuts equally between 2 elephants. How many peanuts each?
How many left over?

Share 9 balloons equally between 3 clowns.
How many balloons each?

Which is right?

Circle the problems whose answers match
the numbers at the top of each box.

3
6 ÷ 3
22 ÷ 2
25 ÷ 5
27 ÷ 9

10
12 ÷ 4
32 ÷ 8
60 ÷ 6
10 ÷ 5

8
64 ÷ 8
72 ÷ 12
18 ÷ 6
81 ÷ 9

4
36 ÷ 9
20 ÷ 2
16 ÷ 8
12 ÷ 4

6
50 ÷ 10
96 ÷ 12
18 ÷ 9
24 ÷ 4

7
88 ÷ 11
28 ÷ 4
12 ÷ 6
72 ÷ 9

Division test

Do the division and write the answers in the boxes.
Check your answers by looking back at the division tables.

$6 \div 3 =$ ☐

$14 \div 2 =$ ☐

$25 \div 5 =$ ☐

$27 \div 9 =$ ☐

$4 \div 2 =$ ☐

$32 \div 8 =$ ☐

$40 \div 4 =$ ☐

$5 \div 5 =$ ☐

$21 \div 7 =$ ☐

$8 \div 2 =$ ☐

$9 \div 1 =$ ☐

$44 \div 11 =$ ☐

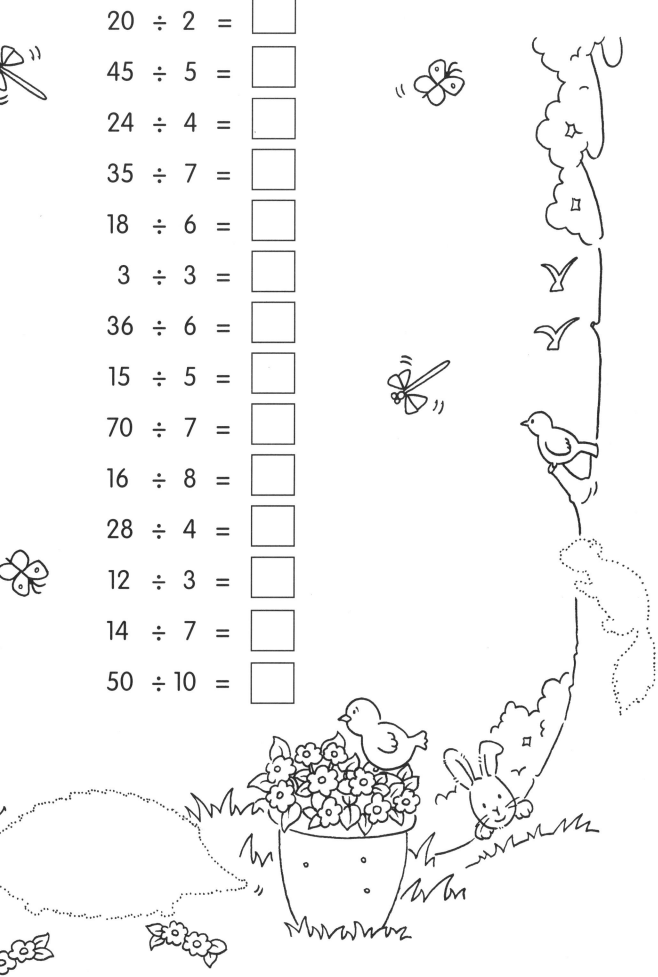

$20 \div 2 =$ ☐

$45 \div 5 =$ ☐

$24 \div 4 =$ ☐

$35 \div 7 =$ ☐

$18 \div 6 =$ ☐

$3 \div 3 =$ ☐

$36 \div 6 =$ ☐

$15 \div 5 =$ ☐

$70 \div 7 =$ ☐

$16 \div 8 =$ ☐

$28 \div 4 =$ ☐

$12 \div 3 =$ ☐

$14 \div 7 =$ ☐

$50 \div 10 =$ ☐

Answers

Math pails
$3 \times 2 = 6$ $5 \times 5 = 25$ $9 \times 6 = 54$

Multiplication problems
$3 \times 8 = 24$ $5 \times 6 = 30$ $7 \times 2 = 14$

Missing numbers
$2 \times 2 = 4$	$3 \times 5 = 15$	$7 \times 2 = 14$
$3 \times 3 = 9$	$6 \times 5 = 30$	$9 \times 2 = 18$
$4 \times 5 = 20$	$1 \times 3 = 3$	$4 \times 4 = 16$
$7 \times 8 = 56$	$2 \times 4 = 8$	$11 \times 3 = 33$
$9 \times 5 = 45$	$6 \times 6 = 36$	$8 \times 3 = 24$
$4 \times 7 = 28$	$12 \times 5 = 60$	$10 \times 3 = 30$
$4 \times 3 = 12$	$1 \times 11 = 11$	$8 \times 5 = 40$
$9 \times 3 = 27$	$8 \times 9 = 72$	$12 \times 12 = 144$
$11 \times 10 = 110$	$6 \times 8 = 48$	$6 \times 4 = 24$
$7 \times 9 = 63$	$2 \times 2 = 4$	$12 \times 8 = 96$
$9 \times 9 = 81$	$3 \times 7 = 21$	

Magical numbers
$3 \times 3 = 9$ $4 \times 6 = 24$ $10 \times 9 = 90$

Match the answers
$7 \times 8 = 56$ $9 \times 9 = 81$ $3 \times 3 = 9$
$5 \times 6 = 30$ $7 \times 3 = 21$ $4 \times 12 = 48$

Missing bees
$3 \times 4 = 12$ $2 \times 3 = 6$ $8 \times 2 = 16$

Flower math
$3 \times 0 = 0$ $3 \times 4 = 12$ $5 \times 2 = 10$

Number puzzles

6	×	2	=	12
×		×		×
3	×	1	=	3
=		=		=
18	×	2	=	36

2	×	5	=	10
×		×		×
2	×	4	=	8
=		=		=
4	×	20	=	80

Number crossword

```
                    8t
                     w
        f o u r 6t e e n
  2e              w    l
   l    5n        o    v
   e     i             e
  1s e v e n t y
         e   e
  9t e n
```

Multiplication test
$2 \times 2 = 4$	$4 \times 5 = 20$	$8 \times 8 = 64$
$1 \times 3 = 3$	$5 \times 8 = 40$	$6 \times 7 = 42$
$11 \times 2 = 22$	$10 \times 10 = 100$	$6 \times 9 = 54$
$3 \times 12 = 36$	$2 \times 8 = 16$	$7 \times 6 = 42$
$5 \times 5 = 25$	$7 \times 12 = 84$	$3 \times 9 = 27$
$4 \times 4 = 16$	$5 \times 6 = 30$	$4 \times 7 = 28$

$9 \times 6 = 54$	$11 \times 11 = 121$	$8 \times 4 = 32$
$12 \times 6 = 72$	$1 \times 9 = 9$	$3 \times 3 = 9$
$6 \times 6 = 36$	$8 \times 3 = 24$	

Juggling math
$6 \div 3 = 2$	$16 \div 2 = 8$	$42 \div 7 = 6$
$24 \div 4 = 6$	$27 \div 3 = 9$	$30 \div 5 = 6$
$9 \div 1 = 9$	$63 \div 9 = 7$	

Missing numbers
$4 \div 4 = 1$	$8 \div 4 = 2$	$21 \div 7 = 3$
$54 \div 6 = 9$	$36 \div 6 = 6$	$63 \div 9 = 7$
$49 \div 7 = 7$	$99 \div 9 = 11$	$12 \div 6 = 2$
$36 \div 9 = 4$	$9 \div 9 = 1$	$56 \div 7 = 8$
$42 \div 7 = 6$	$18 \div 6 = 3$	$20 \div 4 = 5$
$28 \div 7 = 4$	$24 \div 6 = 4$	$18 \div 9 = 2$
$70 \div 7 = 10$	$99 \div 9 = 11$	$48 \div 6 = 8$
$27 \div 9 = 3$	$32 \div 4 = 8$	$45 \div 9 = 5$
$30 \div 6 = 5$	$10 \div 5 = 2$	$72 \div 8 = 9$
$40 \div 5 = 8$	$90 \div 10 = 9$	$56 \div 8 = 7$
$6 \div 3 = 2$	$24 \div 8 = 3$	

Butterfly math
$6 \div 2 = 3$ $4 \div 2 = 2$ $10 \div 2 = 5$

Star math
$81 \div 9 = 9$	$35 \div 5 = 7$	$49 \div 7 = 7$
$12 \div 6 = 2$	$20 \div 5 = 4$	$3 \div 3 = 1$
$32 \div 4 = 8$	$55 \div 11 = 5$	

Solve these problems
Each child would have 4 books.
Each child would have 2 ice cream cones.
There would be 1 left over.
Each rabbit would have 4 carrots.
Each monkey would have 2 bananas.
Each elephant would have 4 peanuts.
There would be 1 left over.
Each clown would have 3 balloons.

Which is right?
$27 \div 9 = 3$	$60 \div 6 = 10$	$64 \div 8 = 8$
$36 \div 9 = 4$	$24 \div 4 = 6$	$28 \div 4 = 7$

Division test
$6 \div 3 = 2$	$14 \div 2 = 7$	$25 \div 5 = 5$
$27 \div 9 = 3$	$4 \div 2 = 2$	$32 \div 8 = 4$
$40 \div 4 = 10$	$5 \div 5 = 1$	$21 \div 7 = 3$
$8 \div 2 = 4$	$9 \div 1 = 9$	$44 \div 11 = 4$
$20 \div 2 = 10$	$45 \div 5 = 9$	$24 \div 4 = 6$
$35 \div 7 = 5$	$18 \div 6 = 3$	$3 \div 3 = 1$
$36 \div 6 = 6$	$15 \div 5 = 3$	$70 \div 7 = 10$
$16 \div 8 = 2$	$28 \div 4 = 7$	$12 \div 3 = 4$
$14 \div 7 = 2$	$50 \div 10 = 5$	